# CAR CARE

# CAR CARE

**by the editors of Mechanix Illustrated**

arco
New York

Published by ARCO PUBLISHING COMPANY, INC.
219 Park Avenue South  New York, N.Y. 10003

Fifth Printing, 1974

Library of Congress Catalog Card Number 71-75362
Standard Book Number 668-01918-2

Printed in the United States of America

# CONTENTS

Special Tools You Should Have . . . . . . 6
Spark Plugs—Clue to Engine Behavior. . 10
Lubrication You Do Yourself . . . . . . . 13
On Buying Junkyard Parts . . . . . . . . . 16
How to Be Your Own Safety Inspector. 20
How to Get More Miles Per Tire . . . . . 24
Carb Care . . . . . . . . . . . . . . . . . 28
The Facts on Front Drive . . . . . . . . . . 32
Easy Way to Get 10 Extra Horsepower 36
Give Your Car a $40 Paint Job . . . . . 40
Auto Air Conditioner . . . . . . . . . . . 44
Taking Care of an Air-Cooled Engine. . 48
10 Point Check List for Back Yard
    Mechanics . . . . . . . . . . . . . . . 52
Give Your Car a $10 Physical . . . . . . 55
The Real Story on Gauges . . . . . . . . . 59
A Valve Job for $20 . . . . . . . . . . . . 62
The Trouble With Alternators . . . . . . . 66
Installing Your Own Seat Covers . . . . . 69
Driving Habits Can Ruin Your Car . . . 72
What to Do When a Car Won't Start. . 76
Reline Your Own Brakes . . . . . . . . . . 80
Bolt-On Horsepower . . . . . . . . . . . . 83
When Your Water Pump Doesn't Pump 87
The New Story on Tappets . . . . . . . . 90
Servicing Power Brakes and
    Power Steering . . . . . . . . . . . . . 94
Do You Want to Sell Your Car? . . . . . 98
The Facts on Filters . . . . . . . . . . . . .102
Make Your Car Really Theft Proof! . . .106
Six-Step Spring Tune-Up . . . . . . . . . .109

# SPECIAL TOOLS

MOST week-end mechanics have become so used to doing jobs the hard way that they think it's the name of the game. Well, it's true that no Saturday wrench twirler can stock his garage with the expensive equipment that makes the professional's work so much easier, faster and safer.

But it's also true that there's no reason for the week-ender to risk life and

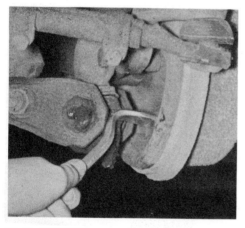

IT IS NEARLY impossible to adjust brakes unless you have this special tool for taking up or else backing off on the star wheel.

limb and spend untold hours on jobs professionals breeze through. A lot is available to make the backyard mechanic's job somewhat easier, and at prices that fit his budget. More specifically, there are ten tools that you might find useful (six of the ten are pictured on these pages).

*First*—We all admire courage, but to lie under a car held up by a bumper jack is madness. The bumper jack just isn't that dependable (and the bumper itself isn't much better). A pit, a lift or even a hydraulic floor jack is just too costly. But there are two other possibilities,

both relatively inexpensive.

One is a set of portable ramps priced at under $30. All one has to do is drive the front or rear of the car onto them. They provide all the clearance anyone needs to grease the chassis, change oil and filter, replace muffler, etc.

The other alternative is a pair of safety stands available for under $15. To use them, just jack up the car and place the safety stands (which are adjustable for height) at appropriate points. A crossmember or the lower A-frames are suitable at the front; at the rear the axle shaft tubes are fine.

**Frozen nuts or bolts** and stuck mufflers and exhaust piping are common headaches for the week-ender. The professional, on the other hand, simply uses his pneumatic chisel or impact wrench. In a matter of seconds, the job is done.

For two reasons, however, pneumatic equipment generally is out of the question for the week-end mechanic: the equipment itself is expensive and it's necessary to have an air compressor to operate it.

SAFETY STANDS should be at the top of your must-buy list. Almost all available models provide adjustment for height.

# YOU SHOULD HAVE

But three specially-designed tools, which cost a total of only $17, can solve most of these problems.

*Second*—a manual version of the impact wrench, at $6.50, is one labor-saver. Available in ½- or ⅜-in. drive, it takes a socket at one end. Just put the tool on the offending nut or bolt and whack the other end with a hammer.

A couple of good shots with the hammer and the most stubborn nut or bolt will give. And if you want to snug down a nut or bolt good and tight, the tool can be set up for this purpose.

SPRING-TYPE hose clamps are other items that often cause hair-pulling and nasty mutterings. Avoid both with a simple tool.

*Third*—If a nut is frozen to a bolt or stud (and penetrating oil can't free it) the nutcracker is the answer. Priced at $8, it's a clamping device with a chisel edge. A hex-head turn-screw (over which a wrench fits) tightens the clamp. The chisel edge will split the nut without damaging the threads of the bolt or

stud on which it's frozen.

*Fourth*—A muffler crowbar, at $2.60, could pay for itself on one job. It has a curved spoon end with a neck for hammering so that it can be driven between

INTERIOR handles must come off on some occasions. But right way to get them off is with tool made for your particular auto.

muffler and pipe (or between two pipes) without damaging either part. Yank on the 11-in. shank of the crowbar to break a rust bond.

**Bleeding brakes** when there's no one around to pump the brake pedal is a common problem for both the weekend and pro mechanic. The pro has to do it every day and his solution is an expensive system that pressurizes the master cylinder.

There's also a method for the backyarder who finds himself without help. It isn't as convenient as the pressurizing system and it does take longer but it costs only a dollar and it does work.

*Fifth*—The low-price answer is a special hose with a ball-check valve you attach to the wheel cylinder bleeder valve. Start by pumping up the brake pedal. Then attach the hose to the bleeder valve, crack open the bleeder valve and hit the brake pedal.

Air (and some brake fluid, of course) will be pushed through the hose, forcing open the check valve and allowing the air to escape As soon as the brake pedal is released the check valve shuts and prevents air from getting back in. Close the bleeder valve and remove the hose, which then can be switched to another wheel cylinder. Or you can buy four hoses, one for each wheel, and make things easier.

*Sixth*—If you've ever tried to pull an inside door handle (to replace the door upholstery, window regulator, glass, etc.), you've probably attacked the job with screwdrivers, crowbars, chisels and just about everything else in the toolbox. Perhaps you gave up. Even if you succeeded, you probably spent a long, aggravating time.

Professionals use specially-shaped tools that cut the job down to a one-minute affair. You can use exactly the same type of tools, because the most expensive of them can be bought for less than a dollar. Less than $4 will cover the tools for most cars but you don't really have to go for more than the one tool designed for the car you own.

*Seventh*—Ever run into a stuck battery-cable terminal? The old twist-and-pry technique probably has broken off more cable terminals and battery posts than all other causes combined.

Yet only $1.75 buys a simple cable-terminal puller. Slip the body of the tool under the terminal and turn a handle-

NUT CRACKER quickly removes frozen nuts. Just turn the hex-head screw and the chisel edge cracks the nut without damaging bolt.

operated screw. The screw exerts downward pressure on the battery post and forces the tool body up, pulling the cable terminal with it.

*Eighth*—Removing and replacing a spark plug in cramped quarters under the exhaust manifold of a modern V-8 has to rank with life's nearly unbearable difficulties. There isn't much you can do about the removal part of the job but a $1.20 tool can help get the plug back in. It's a seven-in. hollow-tube device with spring-loaded steel claws that grip the plug. The tool permits you to start the plug without trying to wedge your fingers under the manifold.

Because of its narrow diameter, the tool can be wiggled in places that defy the socket wrench and extension rod.

BRAKE BLEEDER makes it possible for you to bleed brakes even if no one is around to pump the pedal. One is all you'll need.

A SPECIAL adapter for pressure-flushing a cooling system is a dummy radiator cap and coupling which takes a garden hose.

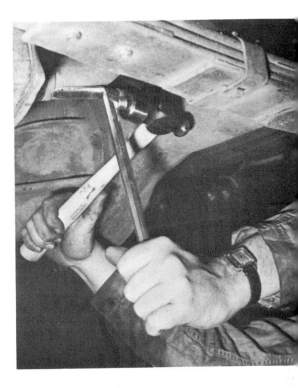

A MUFFLER crowbar has a curved spoon end with a neck for hammering so it can be driven between pipes without damage.

Once the plug is started, just pull a handle to release the claws from the plug.

*Ninth*—Trying to remove spring-type hose clamps with an ordinary pair of pliers is like trying to clip your nails with garden shears—it's the long, wrong way to do it and results will be less than satisfactory.

The special pliers made for the job can be purchased for as little as $1.50. If your car has spring-type hose clamps, the money represents a solid investment. (There also is a similar type of tool for the removal of circlips, or snap rings.)

If you're feeling a bit flush, you might consider buying the special pliers with the built-in tubing cutter wheels. They sell for anywhere from about $3 up, and they're handy for all sorts of jobs, including installation of a fuel line filter kit (this requires cutting out a section of fuel line).

*Tenth*—One of those simple but nice ideas is a $1.30 special adapter for pressure-flushing cooling systems. It's nothing more than a dummy radiator cap with a coupling for a garden hose.

Install it in place of the radiator cap, disconnect the upper radiator hose at the radiator and plug the radiator hose neck with a stopper. Connect the garden hose to the dummy cap, turn on the water and it's all systems go.

Water under pressure courses through the dummy cap into the radiator, through the lower radiator hose into the engine and out the upper radiator hose. Tests have shown this to be an effective way of flushing the cooling system without pulling drain plugs (which usually are frozen in place).

Last, but not least, one of the most important tools in your kit should be a brake adjusting tool or star wheel adjuster. This tool has a bend on one side for taking up on the star wheel and somewhat shallower bend for backing off the brake adjusting nut. Don't try to use a screwdriver, unless you bend the shank first, otherwise you will only chew up the star wheel. Such tools, as well as many of the other specialty tools described, are made by the K-D Mfg. Co., in Lancaster, Pa. and the Milbar Co. in Cleveland, Ohio. •

# SPARK PLUGS:
## Clue to Engine Behavior

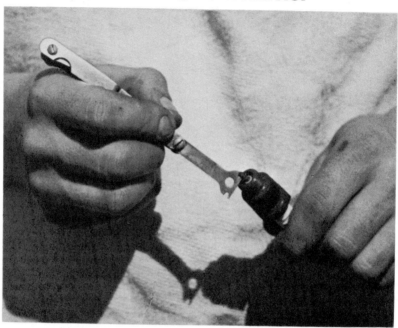

UNLESS each spark plug ignites the fuel-air mixture at precisely the right time and with maximum voltage you are losing power, wasting gasoline and putting an extra load on your ignition system.

Each plug needs periodic servicing or replacement not only because of the hard work it does (15 million sparks each 10,000 mi.), but because of the role it plays in keeping ignition reserve high.

Ignition reserve is the voltage available in the system after a good spark. Reserve is increased if all ignition parts are functioning at their best—that is, if voltage available is high and voltage required low. As plugs wear, foul and lose their gap settings, voltage needs go up and ignition reserve shrinks. When more voltage is needed than the ignition system can produce, it's time for the tow truck.

While modern engines keep spark plugs pretty much out of sight, don't keep them out of mind for servicing every 5,000 mi. Basic tools are a deep socket wrench, extensions and a ratchet. A socket with a neoprene ring that grips the plug is quite useful for hard-to-reach plug holes on modern engines.

**Visual inspection** of the plugs after removal is the most important part of the procedure. Each plug has a story. The type of electrode wear, fouling or damage can tell you how suitable the plugs are for your type of driving and how efficiently the engine is operating.

Arranging the plugs in the same order they occupy in the engine can tell what's going on inside your power plant. If one or two plugs show a different condition than the rest, the cylinders they came out of may be a tip-off to potential trouble.

Under normal conditions electrodes

TWO ADJACENT PLUGS FOULED
POSSIBLE CAUSE: A BLOWN HEAD GASKET

TWO CENTER PLUGS FOULED
POSSIBLE CAUSE: EXTRA-RICH FUEL

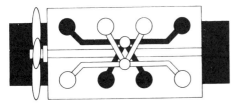

FOUR PLUGS CARBON FOULED AS SHOWN
POSSIBLE CAUSE: UNBALANCED MANIFOLD DISTRIBUTION

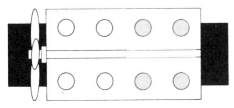

FOUR OVERHEATED IN THE REAR
POSSIBLE CAUSE: POOR WATER CIRCULATION

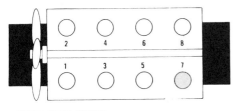

FIRING ORDER 18436572

ONE PLUG OVERHEATED
POSSIBLE CAUSE: CROSS FIRE BETWEEN No. 5 AND No. 6

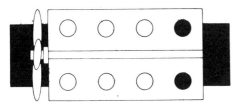

TWO REAR PLUGS OIL FOULED
POSSIBLE CAUSE: OIL PULLED AROUND
INTAKE VALVES DUE TO
PLUGGED DRAIN HOLES
IN CYLINDER HEAD

gradually wear from the destructive action of the spark, heat and combustion pressures. Heavy erosion and a blistered insulator nose are signs of excessive wear, conditions possibly caused by poor coolant circulation, pinging or a too-hot plug.

**Heat range probably is** the most misunderstood feature of spark plugs. It refers to the ability of a plug to conduct heat away from the firing tip. A *hot* plug transfers heat *slowly*—the tip remains hot. A *cool* plug transfers heat *rapidly*—so the tip runs cool. The type of plug you want depends on driving habits.

An engine used in the city with stop-and-go traffic builds up plug deposits from running rich with low combustion-chamber temperatures. A hot plug helps burn away this accumulation. Conversely, a car driven daily on turnpikes runs with high combustion-chamber temperatures calls for a cool plug to carry off the heat.

**There are three types** of fouling deposits that may be found on the firing tip. Each affects engine performance.

Lead fouling is a normal by-product of combustion. Metallic particles colored white, red, brown or yellow accumulate at low engine speeds but pose no problem. At high speeds, however, heat turns the particles into a glazed solid that conducts electricity. Then, as current leaks across the electrodes, operating-temperature and voltage requirements go up, causing preignition and engine miss. Cleaning can remove lead fouling. But if the buildup is packed between insulator and shell, replace the plug. Extended-tip plugs are claimed to run hot enough at low speeds to burn off lead fouling and cool enough at high speeds to prevent miss.

Fuel fouling is indicated by dry, soft, sooty deposits resulting from rich fuel-air mixtures. Check for carburetor flooding or a sticking choke. Plugs too cold for stop-and-go driving are another cause. Clean and regap the plugs. If the condition returns after the carburetor and choke are set correctly, switch to a hotter plug.

Oil fouling shows up as a wet, black deposit and indicates engine wear with oil pumping into the combustion chamber. Switching to a special plug that fires under such conditions holds off fouling but only engine work can seal the combustion chamber. In most cases an oil-fouled plug can be cleaned but if oil deposits are baked hard, replace with a hotter plug.

Plug damage often is caused by mishandling. Breaks in the lower end of the insulator can be made by attempts to bend the center electrode for gap adjustment or by using the center wire as a pivot point to adjust the side tip. Damaged shells or distorted threads result from overtightening.

**After inspection you must decide** whether to replace your plugs. If they are less than 10,000 mi. old, in the correct heat range and undamaged, they can easily be cleaned, gapped and used again.

First clean the top insulators of all plugs and their terminals with a cloth dipped in gasoline. If the lower end is oily, clean it by brushing on the gas and allowing it to dry. Clean the firing tip with gas and a stiff bristle (not wire!) brush. An old toothbrush is fine.

Brush the threads, too.

Be sure to file the center electrode of each plug *flat*. Normal use rounds off the tip, raising voltage requirements for firing.

To measure electrode gap, a round or wire-type gauge is preferable. A flat feeler strip cannot account for irregularities under the side electrode in a used plug.

To set the gap, bend the *side* electrode with the slotted bending jig attached to most spark-gap gauges. Never attempt to adjust the center electrode.

Because the spark-plug gasket has the double task of helping absorb heat from the combustion chamber and maintaining a gas-tight seal at the plug seat, a fresh gasket should be used even when replacing a used plug.

There are a few exceptions. Some Chrysler V8s need no gaskets because the plug sits at the bottom of a deep well within a steel tube that serves as a gasket. And some new plug designs have a taper under the shell that seals as it seats.

A torque wrench is best for tightening the plugs. Recommended torques are 15 ft.-lbs. for 10mm plugs; 30 ft.-lbs. for 14mm; 40 ft.-lbs. for 18mm and 45 ft.-lbs. for ⅞-in. pipe-size plugs. Engines with aluminum heads get 5 ft.-lbs. less.

If you haven't a torque wrench, tighten the plug ½ to ¾ of a turn after it is seated by hand.

Then wipe all insulators with a clean rag before installing the wires. This helps prevent voltage leaks caused by contamination of the rubber boots.

New plugs cost $1 to $1.25 for major brands. Rebuilt plugs often sell for less than half this. Although they are in much better shape than the plugs you've just pulled out of the engine, their life span is shorter than a factory-fresh new plug.

There is a popular misbelief that new plugs need not be checked because they are pregapped at the factory. This may be risky. One plug number usually applies to many engines. Since gap size depends on compression ratio, combustion-chamber design and ignition system requirements, it is impossible for the plug maker to set the gap to satisfy all engines. Gaps set too close produce rough idle; wide gaps cause misfire under load. Always check the specs for your car. •

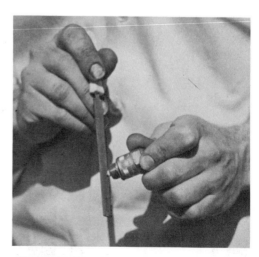

**ALWAYS file the center electrode flat so that the plug needs less voltage to fire.**

# LUBRICATION
## You Do
## Yourself

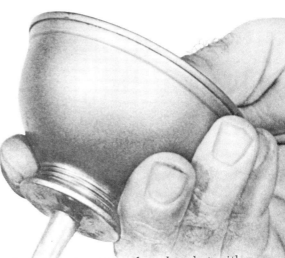

OIL CANS may seem as out-of-date as running boards, what with push-button lubrication, sealed grease fittings and super service stations. But, take my word for it, the lube job you get at the corner station just isn't enough. The guy with the grease gun may be great for transmissions and differentials but rarely does he pick up a common oil can to put a few drops in creaking joints. As a result, your car can go to pot with the speed of greased lightning. And if the man with the gun won't do it, you must.

Oil cans come in all shapes and sizes, including the versatile aerosol bomb. But it's what comes out of the can that counts. There are special oils to provide lubrication for everything from a noisy generator belt to weather-stripping around doors. Far too many seemingly well-serviced cars literally are starving for such treatment.

**Want to be an expert** at the auxiliary oiling that will give your car many added miles of top service? Want to get rid of a lot of car problems that are not checked with a standard grease job? Want to forestall costly repairs with the aid of remedial lubricants? Then get yourself an oil can.

Because such major chassis parts as ball joints and steering connections are sealed for 30,000 miles of service (in theory at least) there's been wholesale neglect of other parts which need frequent attention. The ignition distributor is one. So are the front-wheel bearings. Also likely to be overlooked is the generator, which requires a few drops of light engine oil at regular intervals.

**Lubrication of the** distributor must be precise. Usually there is an oiler outside the distributor into which should be put three to five drops of SAE 10W oil every 1,000 miles. There's a felt pad under the rotor in the top of the distributor and this requires the same amount of lubricant. After wiping the old lube from the surface of the cam apply a light film of petroleum jelly or special cam grease. Avoid overdoing it. Excess lube that is thrown from the cam will get on the points and cause arcing and burning.

For years motorists have been warned against oiling exposed carburetor parts. As a result there has been excessive wear here as well as faulty action. The main thing is to keep throttle parts clean. A solvent such as Gumout Automatic Choke Cleaner is most effective. Some experienced wheel twirlers apply a graphite and alcohol solution. Another alternative is to use a combination solvent and lubricant, such as Part-Ease, which cleans as well as oils.

When conditioning the automatic choke remove the air cleaner and squirt choke cleaner on both ends of the choke-plate's shaft while opening and closing the valve manually. Also remove the cover from the choke-control's thermostatic coil, replace the air cleaner, start up the engine and squirt choke cleaner into the vacuum cylinder. Such solvents are flammable and should be used carefully. Avoid getting any on the car's finish.

**Using soluble oil** as a rust inhibitor for the cooling system is effective in oiling the water pump internally. In fact, regular applications should make it unnecessary to replace this hard-working unit for the life of the car.

New is use of Wynn's Concentrate for the power-steering system to check that annoying squawk heard when the pressure-relief valve opens as you cut the front wheels to extreme position and accelerate the engine—when parking, for example. Wynn's engineers say the noise is due largely to the relief valve not opening freely.

Solvents, with or without graphite, should be used on a sticking exhaust-manifold heat-control valve. Periodic attention will insure against stickage. While it is possible to reach this valve on most cars with the hood up, it is more logical to attend to it when the car is on a lift for greasing or an oil change. Here you can get at both ends of the shaft and rotate it to help the solvent and lube get to the seat of corrosion. Do this when the valve is cool and tap the ends of the shaft lightly.

While the car is on the lift, use a combination rubber lubricant and cleaner to eliminate squeaks from rubber bushings, shock absorber and stabilizer linkage, grommets and shackles. Ru-Glyde, made by the American Grease

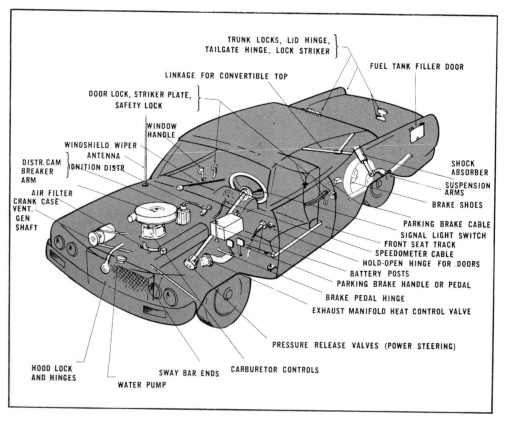

Stick Co., is designed especially for such auxiliary lubrication. You can put it into one of those oil cans with a long snout and a pump handle so as to be able to reach into remote spots.

That grunting so often heard when the car goes into a deep dip in the road usually can be silenced by using rubber lube on the rear suspension arms and bushings. Old lube and grime should be removed first. *Don't overlube.* One theory has it that you should not lubricate rubber parts unless lube is needed as evidenced by noise. Caution: never use mineral (petroleum) oils on rubber parts.

**At the hands of** the average grease monkey, vital parts of the braking system may be overlooked altogether. Brake shoes will operate more smoothly and without noise if they are pried away from the backing plate and the contact surfaces are treated to a thin coating of Bendix or Delco brake lube or Lubriplate. A little of this same lube should be applied to the operating parts of the parking-brake cable and lever.

Dripless oil may be needed on other brake parts, but this should be applied sparingly and with care not to get any on the linings. That hinge for the brake pedal may be corroded and badly in need of freeing but if the pivot shaft for the pedal arm has nylon bushings these should not be treated with cleansing agents nor should they be oiled. This illustrates the importance of having a good working knowledge of your car and its specific lubrication needs. Simply use a clean cloth and wipe the nylon bushings.

In checking the brakes it is not enough to remove dirt and corrosion and to relieve binding. With self-adjusting brakes apply high-temperature grease to the threads as well as to the socket end of the adjusting screw. If the parking-brake handle or pedal does not release fully, correct by cleaning and lubricating the cables and the cable contact areas with a lithium-soap grease.

**So many new parts** require special attention you may be denying the car adequate lubrication even though you go through the motions of chassis greasing more often than the owner's manual suggests. Among the newer points needing attention are the hold-open mechanisms for doors, the little filler door that conceals the fuel-tank cap on many cars, the automatic radio antenna, accelerator linkage for the automatic speed control, tires which may need grounding to wheels with powdered graphite to check radio static, and carburetor air-duct valves.

There's a special cleaner (Gumout PCV) to keep the valve of the positive crankcase ventilation system perking, and if your chariot is equipped with air conditioning don't forget to run this equipment once a week for ten to 15 minutes through the winter to maintain adequate lubrication of moving parts.

Silicone sprays are just the ticket for keeping a long list of car parts in better shape. Such solutions will check battery-post corrosion, improve radio reception when applied to the antenna and silence a noisy speedometer cable.

Stick-type grease has a lot of applications in keeping car body parts operating freely and quietly. Apply it to door strikers, lock-fork bolts and rotors, as well as to the lid-lock bolt of the trunk and the tail-gate hinge and lock striker of a station wagon. Always clean such parts first.

**Go deeper into the trunk** and use Lubriplate on such parts as the lid hinges so that when you unload at a motel other guests won't think you're doing the sound effects for a whodunit. The door-lock cylinder-shaft bell housing also will work better if lubricated lightly.

Uncover the door and window controls on an older car and apply a coating of Lubriplate to the moving parts. The same treatment applied to the tracks for the front seat will insure easier adjustment. Dripless oil should be used on linkage for a convertible top, wiping off any excess.

The oil can *can* be the car owner's best friend. Millions of motorists are paying the penalty for overlooking it. •

# ON BUYING JUNKYARD PARTS...

WHILE buying used parts from a wrecking yard may not be as safe as springing for brand-new ones, it's nice to know that most used-parts lots aren't exactly Las Vegases, either. If you know what to buy and how much to pay you'll always save money for good-as-new repairs—and little gamble about it.

Body parts obviously are the safest items to buy at a junkyard (a term that seems to be losing out to *wrecking yard,* which is considered more couth, though no one mistakes the meaning of the old-fashion name). You see exactly what you're getting and there are no hidden expenses if you install used body parts yourself. If you knock out dents and repaint you even can buy a less-than-perfect panel for still less money. Even if you can't do such work you probably can find a part of the same color and trim. Then just bolt or weld it in place. This is one actual advantage over buying new body parts since new panels usually are painted in primer only.

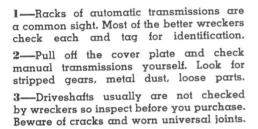

1—Racks of automatic transmissions are a common sight. Most of the better wreckers check each and tag for identification.

2—Pull off the cover plate and check manual transmissions yourself. Look for stripped gears, metal dust, loose parts.

3—Driveshafts usually are not checked by wreckers so inspect before you purchase. Beware of cracks and worn universal joints.

**There's one part,** however, that you always should buy at a wrecking yard— a door. In addition to offering a possible color match, the wrecker's door will be complete with windows, regulating mechanisms and inside upholstery.

Unlike body parts, mechanical and electrical components involve some risk. But, although the wrecker won't offer any extended or written guarantees, he usually will exchange any component that fails in a short time. The definition of short time varies but a starter or generator should last more than a few weeks; a major power train component more than a month.

On most cars, starters, generators, power steering pumps, steering boxes, carburetors, radiators, brake-system components, fuel pumps, etc., are reasonably easy to install. Or at least they don't require the use of a lift or other special equipment—which means the job can be done in your backyard on a Saturday.

Engines, transmissions, driveshafts and rear axles demand reasonably good garage equipment to install safely. So if you're borrowing or renting the necessary equipment and also arranging for a helper you want reasonable assurance that the component will work.

**Wrecking yards recognize** this degree of risk and try to keep it down. After all, their primary customers are professional mechanics who don't want to waste time on fruitless installations. For this reason, most wreckers check out the parts they're selling. Engines are started and run briefly on all but late-model, low-mileage cars, in which the engines are assumed to be good. But on request a wrecker even will start one of those for a customer.

Manual transmissions are checked by engaging the different gears and then pulling the cover plate and looking for chipped gears and gritty grease. These tests generally turn up transmission faults with the exception of worn

IF the part you need is not in stock, ask your friendly wrecker to check with his associates—you may get the part that day.

bearings, so the odds are in your favor.

A carburetor will be checked only for broken hardware and cracked sections. If it's dirty and requires partial disassembly for cleaning that's your responsibility.

**Braking system** components usually are not checked for one of two reasons:

• In the typical wreck the brakes usually are inoperative due to a brake-line fracture or puncture.

• Cylinders and power units are relatively inexpensive to rebuild so there isn't much of a market for used components.

Brake drums and pieces of hardware are the exceptions and these items should be checked carefully.

Automatic transmissions often appear to be high-risk units. The wrecker checks for a cracked case (common on the late-model aluminum transmissions), smells the oil for burn-out and pulls the pan to see if a band is broken or unusually loose. Prices for a late automatic usually run $50 less than the wholesale price of a rebuilt. On older cars the difference may exceed $75. Since late-model automatics usually are reliable the saving justifies the risk. But before you install the unit replace the front and rear seals.

Power steering may or may not be given a quick check before the car is dismantled, depending on the policy of the wrecking yard and the type of accident in which the car was involved.

Small parts, especially for older cars, should be purchased in wrecking yards. If you appear to be mechanically inclined and have your own tools with you, and the wrecked car is anchored, the wrecker may let you pull off what you need. In such situations he'll look at what you've taken and say, "Okay, give me so many dollars for everything." So-many seldom exceeds five, mainly because this arrangement doesn't take up the wrecker's time to pull parts awkward to remove.

**Obviously, there are no** price tags or list prices for used parts. To some people, buying parts from a wrecker is like shopping in a European souvenir shop.

Generally, however, prices on used parts represent the result of fast consideration of the following factors:

• Wholesale price of the new part.

• Wholesale price of a rebuilt part, if available.

• Physical accessibility of the part on a typical wreck.

• General availability in any geographic area of that part—whether new, rebuilt or used. This is a major factor on parts for foreign cars and American high-performance rigs.

• What work is necessary to make the part suitable for reuse. A body panel, for example, will need stripping, sanding and repainting unless the color happens to match. On the other hand, a new panel needs only the finishing coats of paint.

There is, of course, a margin between wholesale and retail prices at wrecking yards. But it's nothing near the normal discount range on new and rebuilt components.

**On a *used-vs-new basis*,** mechanical and electrical assemblies usually are cheaper than body parts, primarily because rebuilts are readily available and the whole discount structure is different. The professional mechanic gets perhaps a 25 per cent discount on body parts, compared with 25 to 60 per cent on electrical and mechanical components. While the amateur mechanic can't get this full discount, some parts-supply houses nevertheless will give the week-end wrench twirler some sort of discount if he bothers to ask for it.

In general, you should pay no more for a body part than 60 per cent of the new list price. For a used mechanical or electrical part, pay half of the rebuilt or a quarter of the new price. Prices for parts of late-model engines will be somewhat higher, running up to 50 per cent of new list. For example, a new starter that lists for $50 may be $30 wholesale. A rebuilt will sell for $25 retail and $12 to 16 wholesale. However, to get the professional to chance a used starter, the wrecker will sell it for $5 to $7, or a bit less than half the price of a rebuilt. Then, even if the used starter fails, the professional will do the job again at no charge to the customer simply because he has enough margin to cover his investment of time and money. Yet because the difference between the price for professional and amateur mechanics is only a couple of dollars the same starter should cost you only $7 to $9.

The primary reason for the fractional margin between professional and amateur prices is simple—any amateur mechanic who buys at a wrecking yard is price-conscious. Also, amateurs sometimes are better customers than professionals. A pro may limit his wrecking-yard purchases to an occasional rear axle, brake drum or wheel. The amateur, however, may buy virtually everything he needs at the wrecking yard, then steer many similarly minded friends to the same place.

**So don't think the wrecker** doesn't want to bother with you. And don't feel that your car has to be a clunker to justify the use of wrecking-yard parts. Visit any wrecking yard and you'll see primarily late model cars.

It might appear that the wrecker's basic pricing policies would insure a bargain. But unfortunately most wreckers follow a standard price technique. That is, all starters are $9, all generators are $8 and so on (except for the really unusual units, such as parts for foreign and high-performance cars).

It may be that the particular unit you need is low-priced to start with. But if you walk into the wrecking yard knowing how much the part would cost new or rebuilt you will avoid overpaying. If you point out that the part normally is in the unusually-low-price class the average wrecker will knock off a few dollars.

**Can you haggle** over prices with a wrecker? Yes, but—parts prices for late-model cars usually are not subject to bargaining. But they invariably are for parts of cars five years old or older. Remember that the older car likely costs the wrecker little and the market for its innards declines every day.

The exception to the rule is an unusually busy yard. When the place is packed with people clamoring for parts there's just no time to deal. The typical yard is busiest on Saturday (when most week-end mechanics come in) but slowest early mornings and late afternoons during the week.

**Consider trading** if you're short on cash. You might try offering the wrecker that old Jeep transmission that's just sitting in your garage. Some wreckers won't be the least bit interested. As one put it, "Whatever the average guy wants to trade, I've already got 20 of." But another commented, "You bet! I sell a lot of performance parts, and I pick up a lot of offbeat stuff on trades." So try swapping for the parts you need. You even might be lucky enough to drive away with both extra cash and a trunk full of spare parts.

Always ask the wrecker for a receipt, especially if you're buying a part that might be defective. Although the typical wrecker is honest about making exchanges he may not remember your face from among the thousand he sees every week. The receipt eliminates most arguments.

But don't expect the wrecker to make good on your mistakes. A wrecker who's asked to exchange a generator that looks as if it just came out of a crematorium is going to blame you or your regulator. For, although a wrecker won't stay in business by pawning off defective parts, he also won't last long by playing the soft touch. •

# how to be your own

# SAFETY

TWIST each wheel vertically. Excessive motion means bad wheel bearing or kingpin.

SPRUNG doors can be fixed by realigning lock catch on jamb—a matter of minutes.

WHETHER your car sports a safety-inspection sticker or simply doesn't require inspection by state law, the actual responsibility of its condition lies with you and you alone.

A few simple checks, a mind alert to danger signs and periodic maintenance —that's all it takes to be a good safety inspector. And here's how to go about your inspections:

**The lighting system** commonly is neglected by otherwise-careful motorists. Almost any night you're sure to see at least one car with a burned-out headlight or taillight. A single headlight approaching near the center of a narrow road always starts me wondering—is it the left or the right light or is it a motorcycle?

Checking headlights, parking lights and taillights is a straightforward operation. Just switch them on and walk around the car. Check both the high and low beams on headlights since usually just one filament burns out.

Checking the stoplights doesn't always require an assistant to press the brake pedal. After dark (or in a darkened garage), back up close to a wall, step on the brake pedal and watch for two red reflections. Directionals also can be checked this way, or by watching your dashboard pilot light. When a bulb isn't lighting the pilot either will stay lit without flashing or it won't go on at all.

When a light doesn't work the bulb or sealed-beam lamp usually is to blame. However, corrosion in the socket sometimes prevents electrical contact so check this before replacing the lamp.

Many motorists carry a spare bulb and sealed beam in the trunk but not only for the obvious safety reasons. If a light burns out without their knowledge

# INSPECTOR

STEERING wheel should have some play but more than two in. means bad linkage.

SEARCH for exhaust leaks by stuffing a rag in tailpipe, then looking underneath for puffs.

and a policeman stops them, offering to change the bad bulb on the spot may save them from a ticket.

The fact that your headlights are on isn't enough. They have to be aimed to light the road without dazzling oncoming traffic. Have your headlight alignment checked twice a year and whenever you replace a sealed-beam lamp. A quick test is to shine your high beams on a wall about 20 ft. away. Both reflections should be dead ahead and at the same height from the ground as the headlights. If one reflection is lower, get your lights reaimed. The same advice holds if your headlights don't seem to be lighting the road as well as they used to or if approaching cars often flash their high beams at you when you're driving on low beams.

**Other safety details** are worth a fast check. A sprung door, for instance, could fly open in a minor collision. Fix it by loosening the screws that hold the lock catch on the door jamb, then reposition the catch to make proper contact with the lock bolt in the car door.

Torn carpeting or rubber matting can tangle around a foot, while a worn or missing pedal cover can cause your shoe to slip off the pedal.

Your horn is another important safety device. Toot it once in awhile (preferably when no traffic is nearby) to make sure it's working.

A driver's seat that's loose on its track can shift unexpectedly and cause you to lose control. And loose or badly corroded seat-belt hardware could cause belt failure in an accident. All these are short checks and all are important.

**Good visibility** is a matter of common sense but a surprising number of motorists forget periodically to wipe their

# SAFETY INSPECTOR

BRAKE-FLUID reservoir usually is under hood. Any loss of fluid should be checked.

INSPECT tire treads often. Remove pebbles, nails, etc., that might later cause blowouts.

WHEN brake linings are thickness of a dime or rivet heads are exposed, get new linings.

windshields. This can create serious glare, especially when the sun is low or when you face oncoming headlights. Headlights and taillights also should be clean. Dust cuts brilliance drastically.

On many cars, dashboard glare is another problem. Either spray the dashboard with a dark, dull finish or cut a cover from pressure-sensitive dark felt and secure it to the dash. Before you set out on a long trip, wax your hood and cowl but don't buff them. The dull finish will cut reflections and make driving more pleasant. Get rid of any clutter on the rear shelf. You might scrape off all those unofficial stickers on your windows, too.

Windshield wipers are another much-neglected item. Temperature changes and exposure to sunlight can make the rubber in the blades brittle, causing smearing and even scoring of the glass. Replace the blades every spring and fall. And be sure your wipers run fast enough and the arms have enough spring tension.

**So much for the easy checks.** Let's now examine two of the most critical components in your car, the brakes and steering. You often hear drivers involved in an accident offer the excuse: "I stepped on the brakes but nothing happened." Perhaps their brakes did fail without warning. But more often than not these drivers just didn't pay attention to one or more little telltale clues.

A spongy pedal, for example, indicates air in the brake lines, which must be bled.

A low brake pedal, one with more than an inch of free play, means adjustment is needed to take up lining wear. This should be done twice a year. Swerving to one side either means that adjustment is needed or that one or more of the linings is contaminated with a foreign substance such as grease. A slight swerve under normal driving conditions could become a dangerous skid during a panic stop.

Another danger sign is a drop in hydraulic-fluid level. The fluid reservoir in most cars is in the engine compartment. To check the level, just unscrew the cap after first cleaning away the dirt.

If you have to add much fluid, or even if you regularly have to add a little, suspect a leak somewhere in the brake lines, master cylinder or wheel cylinders. This requires immediate attention, since a tiny leak can suddenly enlarge and drop all your fluid. To inspect your brake system for signs of leaks, check around seals and brake-line connections. Also make sure the lines aren't chafing against the chassis.

Most cars must be jacked up to inspect the brake system because of low ground clearance. But don't trust the jack alone—a couple of sturdy jack stands are a good investment for the do-it-yourself safety inspector.

The hand brake also should be inspected. The lever, whether hand- or foot-operated, usually works on a ratchet principle. If more than five clicks of the ratchet mechanism are heard before the brake is set fully, get an adjustment.

While you're under the car, check the exhaust system. A leak here could allow deadly carbon-monoxide fumes to seep into the passenger compartment. Also inspect the tightness of all exhaust fittings. A hot muffler or tailpipe, if it should fall off at 60 mph, will present quite a hazard to cars behind.

Before climbing from under the car, check the inner sidewalls on your tires for cuts or bulges. Also check the suspension system for broken springs or loose U-bolts. A collapsed suspension at high speed could give you some exciting moments.

With the front end jacked up, grasp each front tire firmly at the top and bottom and try to twist the wheel from top to bottom. There should be little or no motion. If the wheel does move but the brake backing plate doesn't the wheel bearing probably is worn. If the backing plate moves with the wheel, blame the kingpin or ball joint.

Brake linings should be checked for wear after 12,000 mi. and at periodic intervals thereafter—even if the brakes seem to be working properly. To check your brake linings it's only necessary to pull one of the front wheels. This is because the front gets more punishment due to more front-end weight and even more weight transfer from the car's momentum. The only exception is if you suspect that a mechanical defect may have worn down the rear linings prematurely.

Few people realize how easy it is to check brake linings. Remove the hub-cap to expose the axle hub. Most cars have a dust cap on the end of the hub, which should be pried off with a screwdriver. Then pull out the cotter pin that passes through the hub, slide off the cotter-pin key and unscrew the retaining nut. Carefully remove the wheel bearing, the wheel and the brake-drum assembly, leaving the brake linings exposed. On a few cars, such as late-model Chevrolets, you don't have to disassemble the hub.

If the lining is riveted to the shoe, be sure the rivet heads are well below the surface of the lining. If the lining is bonded, replace it when its thickness is about that of a dime. When you replace the hub parts, *always use a new cotter pin*.

Checking disc-brake pads is even easier. Undo the wheel studs and remove the wheel. You'll then be able to see the thickness of the pads. (On a few cars you will have to remove the splash shield to view the pads.)

**The steering mechanism** is another crucial component in your car. Check for excessive wear of steering linkage by measuring steering-wheel play at the rim. With the front wheels resting on the ground, turn the steering wheel left and right until you feel slight resistance at both ends. If this wheel movement measures more than two inches, your steering system needs attention.

If you're driving and the car pulls in either direction or the front end shimmies sideways, a likely cause is misaligned front wheels. An up-and-down vibration of front end and a corresponding vibration in steering wheel indicates out-of-balance front wheels.

You checked the inner sidewalls on your tires when you were underneath the car. Now inspect the outer sidewalls and treads. A couple of common booby traps to watch out for are improper inflation and uneven tread wear. And remember, check tire pressure weekly. •

# HOW TO GET MORE MILES PER TIRE

A NEIGHBOR recently complained that one of his four new premium-quality tires had blown out after less than 8,000 miles. After a glance at the other three bulging, unevenly-worn tires, we had to concede he was lucky.

He had avoided an accident—his neglect would only cost him the price of four new tires. Yet with a bit of simple preventive maintenance and common sense, he probably could have avoided this disconcerting incident and tripled his tire life.

My neighbor isn't too unusual. Few motorists check their tire pressure once a week. Even fewer own a tire gauge. If you're one of the offenders, get a good, reliable gauge. Don't rely on the one built into the air pump at your service station—many are off by as much as six pounds.

Frequent checking is necessary because even sound tires lose air gradu-

**TOO MUCH PRESSURE** causes center of tread to bulge and wear faster than the edges (tire shown deflated). Also, ride is harsher.

**TOO MUCH CAMBER** (where wheels tilt in or out at the top) will cause uneven wear like this along one side of the tire tread only. Check treads often.

**EXCESSIVELY** worn shoulders mean tires have been underinflated. If only outside edge is worn, you may be too fast on curves and corners.

ally. Also, seasonal temperature changes will affect pressure. For each 10° drop in temperature, tire pressure drops about one lb. Thus, if you don't check your tires from late summer through early winter, you could be running five or six lbs. low.

Take pressure readings only when tires are cold. Highway driving will raise the pressure by several pounds after just a few miles. Never bleed off air after a hard drive to get the reading down—your tires will flex excessively and run hot. Furthermore, they will be badly underinflated when they cool off.

**How much pressure is best?** If you own a new car, your owner's manual is a good guide. Most manufacturers list at least two figures: one for normal driving, and another for carrying heavy loads or for sustained turnpike driving (over 60 mph for an hour or longer). Unfortunately, American manufactur-

ers sometimes recommend pressures that are too low because this makes cars ride softer. It's safe to increase these figures by about four lbs. as long as you don't go over 32 lbs. with four-ply-rating or 40 lbs. with eight-ply-rating tires. You'll hardly notice the firmer ride.

Inflating the tire any higher makes it too stiff, leaving it more susceptible to impact damage from rough roads or obstacles. Also, the center of the tread bulges out and wears faster because the tire's footprint, or contact area, is reduced. Finally, the ride becomes harsh, and both the suspension and you take a beating.

Underinflation is even worse. Then the sidewall is so soft that it flexes with each revolution and builds up heat. This in turn weakens the tire structure and softens the tread rubber. Also, as the tire bulges, the center of the tread tends to lift, promoting faster wear along the

IF TIRE is dragged sideways across the road due to improper alignment of wheels, feathered edges like these will result in short order.

DEFECTS in suspension, brakes, steering or wheel balance can mean irregular wear and cupping. Check now and avoid a blowout.

sides. You also will notice heavier steering, poor road adhesion and more lean on corners.

Some car manufacturers recommend different tire pressures for front and rear tires to make up for unusual weight distribution or suspension design. This differential *must* be observed. Rear-engined cars such as the Corvair and Volkswagen are particularly sensitive to tire pressures. If the rear tires don't carry more air than the front ones, the car develops vicious oversteer—a tendency for the rear end to slide around. If your car has air-conditioning, the extra weight of this accessory calls for a couple of extra pounds in the front tires.

A word of caution: if your car has the new radial-ply tires (as do many foreign cars) don't add air just because they *look* flat. Unlike conventional tires, whose plies are placed opposite each other and at about 40° to the circumference of the tread, radial plies are laid at 90° to the beads, like the stripes around the body of a zebra. A rigid belt strengthens the tread circumference, but the sidewalls are flexible, making the tire look underinflated.

**Overloaded tires** may not be as common as improperly inflated tires, but they are even more dangerous. The original-equipment tires on most new cars can safely carry five or six passengers and a reasonable amount of luggage at legal turnpike speeds. But add a roof rack filled with trunks, or hook on a trailer, and you may be in for trouble.

An overloaded tire also bulges and flexes as it rolls, building up heat. And it is far more vulnerable to impact damage. Overloading also strains the suspension and running gear and hurts handling and braking. If you *must* carry heavy loads, increase the tire pressure. Going from 26 to 32 lbs. can raise each tire's load-limit 100 to 250 lbs., depending on its size. It's always safer, however, to switch to the next larger tire size or to a higher ply rating. In fact, even for normal driving you can increase your safety margin by specifying the next larger size next time you buy a set of replacement tires.

Inspect your tires whenever your car is being serviced on a lift. Turn each wheel with your hands and check the sidewalls for deep cuts, bulges or knots—which could mean separation of the tire tread or possibly the sidewall. If you spot any danger signs, have an expert dismount the tire and examine it on the inside.

**Check for grease marks** on the inner sidewalls and, if necessary, repair any leaking grease seals. Petroleum-base substances such as grease, oil, gas and kerosene are harmful to tires.

If pebbles, glass or nails are imbedded in the tread, carefully pry them out with needle-nose pliers. Removing a nail may let out the air but it's better that this happens at the service station and not on the road.

Check the tread for wear. An easy way is to insert the bottom edge of a quarter into each groove. If you can see any part of the date, you need new tires. Don't try to stretch a few extra miles from those balding tires. According to UniRoyal, 90 per cent of tire failures occur in the last 10 per cent of tread life.

Your tire treads also can tip you off to mechanical problems. For example, when the tread pattern is feathered in one direction, your wheels need to be aligned.

Wear on only one side of a tire indicates excessive camber (where the wheels tilt inward on top as in a knock-kneed stance, or outward as in a bowlegged stance). However, if the wear is on the outside edge, fast cornering may be to blame.

**Irregular wear** or cupping, where a small section of tread is gouged out, could be caused by grabbing brakes or worn shock absorbers. To check your brakes, pick a dry, smooth, open area such as a large parking lot. Accelerate to 20 mph, let go of the steering wheel, and hit the brakes hard. If the car swerves severely, your brakes need attention.

To test shock absorbers, push down hard on each bumper. If the car bounces up then levels immediately, your shocks are good. If it bounces up and down several times, they're faulty.

Other troubles to check for are bad springs, worn wheel bearings, loose steering and tires rubbing on body metal.

Still another cause of irregular wear is an out-of-balance wheel. This can happen even in new cars. An unbalanced front wheel sets up a rotating centrifugal force,

something like a stone being whirled at the end of a string. The resultant hop and vibration isn't noticeable at low speeds, but over 45 or 50 mph it can make you feel as if you're driving a Mixmaster. Rear wheels have no steering freedom, so their unbalance is rarely felt.

The cure for out-of-balance wheels is attaching lead weights in the proper places along the edges of the wheel rim. Though some motorists try to balance their own wheels, it's definitely not recommended.

Many garages have equipment for static wheel balancing. This means simply that a wheel so balanced has no heavy spot. If it were spun on a frictionless hub, it would stop in a different position every time.

**For the best results,** however, you also should get *dynamic* balancing. To understand this, picture a perfectly balanced roller to which you add a weight on one end and another equal weight at the other, but halfway around. The roller now is statically balanced in that it has no preferential stopping position. However, when the roller is spun, the two weights set up centrifugal forces in opposite directions, making the roller wobble from side to side. A wheel rim is narrower than a roller, so the forces, while less pronounced, are nevertheless strong enough to be felt at high speed.

Normal wear is enough to disturb the balance, so wheels should be rebalanced every 10,000 to 15,000 miles.

It's also wise to equalize wear by rotating your wheels every 5,000 miles. Several rotating schemes are recommended by various car manufacturers—any one is good as long as you stick to it. The most common calls for switching the wheels from spare to left front to left rear to right front to right rear.

If one or more tires are worn much more than the others, cornering and braking become erratic. For the same reason, don't mix brands or tread patterns. (The exception is the use of snow or studded tires in winter, of course.) Under no circumstances should two radial-ply tires be used with two conventional tires, since the cornering behavior of the two types differs greatly. •

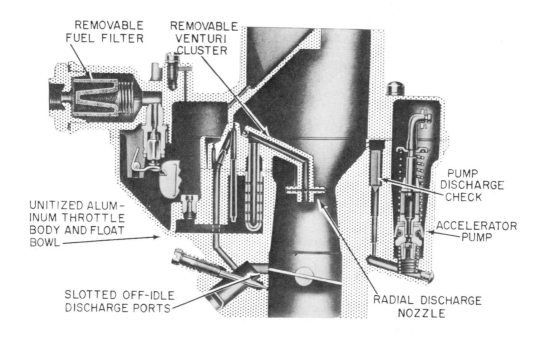

REMOVABLE FUEL FILTER

REMOVABLE VENTURI CLUSTER

PUMP DISCHARGE CHECK

UNITIZED ALUM-INUM THROTTLE BODY AND FLOAT BOWL

ACCELERATOR PUMP

SLOTTED OFF-IDLE DISCHARGE PORTS

RADIAL DISCHARGE NOZZLE

# CARB CARE

THE CARBURETOR is the heart of the engine and subject to many an odd beat. Because it ties in with the fuel-feed system as well as the engine's combustion chambers it is responsive to the least variation in the fuel itself, the behavior of the fuel pump, the air and fuel filters, ignition timing and the engine's cooling system. Being the sum total of the efficiency of these other factors, good carburetion is more than a properly adjusted float level and a healthy inlet valve.

Fortunately, even though the modern carburetor is indeed complicated, there's a lot that the car-owner can do to keep it healthy. Cleanliness is essential. Few parts of the engine tend to get as grimy as this vital unit all but con-

cealed by the air cleaner.

Solvent, brushed or sprayed on the carburetor, will loosen grime. It can be fed to the carburetor with the engine running so as to clean out the jets and fuel passages. And it can be added to the gas periodically to clean out the carburetor while you drive.

For a fast clean-up, disconnect the fuel line at the carburetor and plug it so the pump can't force through any gasoline while you feed solvent directly to the carburetor.

**Next to cleanliness** comes attention to the carburetor's mechanical fitness. Start with a check on the bolts that hold the unit to the intake manifold. Note also the tension and condition of the throttle-return spring. A weak spring

TYPICAL two-throat carb is stripped down and the metal parts are soaked in a solvent.

CLEAN all passages in the metal parts of the carburetor by blasting air through them.

INSPECT the tip of the needle valve for wear. This is a common cause of flooding.

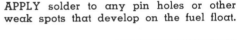

APPLY solder to any pin holes or other weak spots that develop on the fuel float.

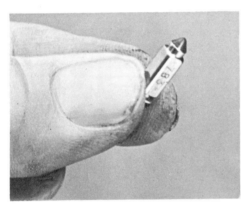

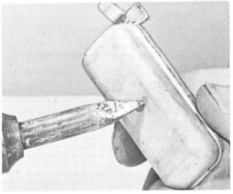

wastes gas; a corroded spring may break.

Note, too, whether the throttle opens fully when the accelerator pedal is pressed to the floor. A bunched-up mat may restrict the pedal's movement and prevent the automatic transmission from being down-shifted for fast passing.

**With the body** of the carburetor clean, it should be easier to detect flooding and to see whether the fast-idle linkage is working as it should. Poor idling often is due merely to need for adjusting the throttle stop. The head of this screw which checks the closing limit of the throttle is subject to wear, a factor that accounts for an engine's tendency to idle slower as miles pile up —unless adjustment is made.

With the air cleaner removed you can see exactly how the choke is operating. Do this first with the engine cold. Press all the way down on the accelerator pedal and then release. The choke valve should then be closed and the fast-idle cam set. Failure of the choke to close may be due to stickage at its shaft, in the linkage or in the choke control on the side of the carburetor. If the choke is the type with a piston, this should be opened and cleaned with solvent. It gets quite gummy.

Next check the choke when the engine is hot. If, after removing the air cleaner, you find that the choke valve is partially closed you may safely conclude that it binds or that the choke control needs adjusting to lean. Failure of the choke to open fully accounts for a lot of delay in restarting hot engines. In all 'cases of hot restarts, hold your foot all the way down on the pedal when cranking. Never pump on the pedal.

Of course, when removing the air cleaner, you will help carburetion by cleaning out the element. Replace a paper element that has seen a lot of mileage. Clogging forces the carburetor to feed more fuel.

**With carburetors available** in single-, dual- and four-barrel forms, as well as in dual-four-barrel and triple-two-barrel versions, it might seem that the complications are too numerous for anything like a popular discourse on the operation, care and feeding of the subject at hand. But there are some guide lines to follow.

Let's take a quick look at a simple carburetor, the main function of which is to mix vaporized gasoline and air. This involves such principles as evaporation, vacuum, atmospheric pressure, volatility of the fuel, atomization and the composition of air.

**There are a number of essentials** to the simplest carburetor mixing process. The one you see first when taking off the air cleaner is the air horn. The big choke valve is located here, but this functions only part time. At the lower portion of the horn there's the hard-working throttle valve, which controls the amount of air allowed to pass through the intake system. En route there's a nozzle through which raw fuel is fed into the horn. Gasoline actually is pushed out of the nozzle by atmospheric pressure. To control this a venturi located just above the nozzle acts like a horn within a horn. A partial vacuum in the venturi's lower area helps to create a fuel-level rise so that gasoline flows from the nozzle as the engine operates.

Other essentials include the float chamber with its float and linkage to open and shut the inlet valve to maintain the fuel supply. There's also a special circuit for idling and low-speed operation.

For acceleration we need a special

SCREW in the idle needle until lightly seated. Make final adjustment at idle speed.

AUTOMATIC choke chamber must be clean, the choke shaft free and the spring intact.

ADJUST the choke by rotating the spring plate until choke butterfly barely closes.

pump which collects an extra slug of raw fuel for injection into the air horn when the driver presses down quickly on the accelerator pedal. This avoids what would otherwise be a flat spot. In addition, there's usually a full-power, vacuum-operated circuit. This involves use of an economizer valve.

There may also be more than one venturi, air bleeds to permit air to bleed into the high-speed nozzle, an antipercolation valve to offset the tendency for fuel to boil in the float chamber because of excessive engine heat, an automatic control for the choke and a throttle cracker to open the throttle slightly during cranking.

**The float system** can be a trouble maker. Its mechanism is subject to wear and the shock of speed changes. Foreign matter will keep the inlet (needle) valve from seating and cause flooding. Use of a special needle valve, like the Viton, stops such flooding because its resilient material permits seating against small particles. You also can use a resilient seat with a regular inlet valve or a resilient free-floating disk such as is offered by Champ-Items.

No matter how much work is done on the carburetor, good results can't be had if this unit is handicapped by such conditions as a clogged exhaust system or intake manifolding that is clogged with gums or leaks air. Cars have an exhaust-manifold heat-control valve or a heat riser to preheat the ingoing mixture when the engine is cold. Check to make sure preheating is taking place. If preheating occurs *after* the warm-up the engine will be sluggish and gas mileage will slide.

Leaky connections or a punctured diaphragm of the vacuum spark control for the ignition distributor not only will affect timing but the calibration of the carburetor itself. And if the car has vacuum-operated windshield wipers, leakage in the lines or in the diaphragm of the booster side of the fuel pump will lean out the mixture excessively. Performance may also be disturbed by faulty action of the dashpot. This is an automatic brake found on the throttle of some cars with automatic transmission to prevent stalling during quick stops.

Many cars have throttle linkage to their automatic transmissions. Improperly adjusted, this linkage will cause incorrect shift points, wasting fuel because of erratic performance.

Often ignored is the engine's thermostat, which is designed to speed the warm-up. Comparatively new is a hot-idle compensator which opens an air valve below the secondary throttle valves automatically to lean the mixture and maintain normal idle speed during prolonged periods of hot idling.

**Before taking** the carburetor to the workbench, observe that the low speed is adjustable by means of one or two idle screws. These may need replacing. In adjusting, have the engine normally hot and running. Turn the screw clockwise until the engine falters as if to stall, then out slightly until it runs fastest. Repeat this several times. Do the same with the second screw if there is one. Then, if the engine idles too fast, cut down at the throttle-stop adjusting screw.

Note that mixture which this circuit provides enters the intake system below the almost closed throttle. There may also be an upper port to supply a little more fuel as the throttle opens for speeds up to 20 mph. However, this phases out as the high-speed circuit comes into action. Details vary so widely here you should not attempt service other than cleaning and replacement of worn parts unless you have precise facts on your particular make and model carburetor.

Good carburetion can't be achieved if valves leak, the engine overheats or ignition isn't up to par.

**For overhauling** the popular makes of carburetors you can buy repair kits for a couple of bucks. A kit will contain an accelerator pump, needle valve and seat and a set of replacement gaskets. I would use one of the speed-float needle valves mentioned earlier, however. A better valve here saves gas by reducing flooding and stalling.

Should you want to replace your present carburetor with a factory-rebuilt job, the exchange price for a carb for a late-model Caddy runs around $23, for a late-model Rambler, $9.50. •

# the Facts on Front Drive

FRONT drive (or front-wheel drive, if you prefer) is with us again on an American-made car. And taking care of the Toronado can be a little like learning sky diving. Thrills abound but much caution is called for.

Taming a Toronado, of course, is nice work if you can get it. Just fooling around under the hood can be a ball. But a wagon so unique has its special points, too.

**Oldsmobile stresses** the need to vary the car's speed during break-in and also recommends short hauls of 25 to 50 mi. If you accelerate and decelerate gradually the engine's moving parts are loaded and unloaded effectively and thus seat better. Olds further advises limiting the Toronado's top speed to 50 mph for the first 100 mi. and 65 mph

for the next 400. Avoid standing starts and a heavy throttle.

After the car has reached the 1,000-mi. mark check that the shift points, up as well as down, conform to the Olds specifications. The carburetor is equipped with a dashpot to slow throttle closing and help prevent stalling on sudden stops. This assembly and the throttle linkage also should be checked carefully.

Toronados delivered in California are equipped with an Air Injection Reactor System to cut exhaust emission of hydrocarbons and carbon monoxide. In this system the engine drives a pump to compress and inject clean filtered air at the exhaust port of each cylinder. The A.I.R. pump's filter should be serviced every 12 months or 12,000 mi. by wash-

ing in kerosene, dipping in SAE 10W-30 oil and squeezing out the excess. The pump itself has a sealed bearing. Stressed is the importance of an annual tune-up to insure the efficiency of the smog-control system.

Toronado's hydraulic brakes have self-adjusters. If there's too much forward driving over a period of time excessive pedal travel will develop. This can be corrected by rocking or driving backwards and forward, applying the brakes at the end of each movement. The mechanical parking-brake system uses an equalizer just behind a rear frame cross-member. With the power brakes there's a built-in vacuum reserve capable of providing two or more assisted stops after the engine has stopped.

Another new item is the horizontal shock absorber which serves to take up the front-end thrust when the driver gooses that 425-cu.-in. mill. This is in addition to the vertical shocks angled between the spring clamps and the frame. In removing a leaf spring the exhaust resonator on the corresponding side has to be loosened and allowed to hang.

Toronado owners will find something unusual in the mufflers and resonators. Each has a small hole in the bottom to drain off condensate. To prevent damage from corrosion be sure to keep the holes clear. An ideal opportunity arises when the Toronado is up on a lift for an oil change (every 6,000 mi. or every six months).

**To compensate** for the concentration of mechanical components under the hood, Olds engineers have aimed at making some of the normal checks as simple as possible. The oil dipstick is at spark-plug level on the driver's side of the car. Just below it is the stick for transmission oil. Check the Turbo Hydra-Matic fluid level as you would on a conventional car (car level, engine warm and idling, selector in Park), remembering that fluid and strainer should be replaced every 24,000 mi. or 24 months. Cut this figure to 12,000 mi. or 12 months if the car is used for a lot of stop-and-go driving.

The front suspension includes a sta-

**Front Drive**

BODY height is increased or decreased just by the turning of a bolt on front-end bar.

SHOCK absorber for the steering system runs from linkage to the front cross member.

HEADLIGHTS can be raised manually. But use care to prevent scratching paint on hood.

REAR wheel bearings should be tightened to 25 to 30 ft.-lbs. and backed off half turn.

bilizer bar as well as torsion-bar springs. Torsion rods mount to the lower control arm and are anchored in a cross-member support to the middle of the car. A feature of this arrangement is that *spring rate can be adjusted by changing the torque on the bars.* (Due to the extremely heavy front-end weight of the Toronado these spring rates range from 540 to 590 lbs. per inch.)

In spite of the front-end weight Olds does not increase front tire pressure. They say it should be the same as for the rear tires— 24 lbs. for up to 750 lbs. of passenger load and 26 lbs. all around for up to 1,100 lbs. of passenger and luggage load. For better road grip or high-speed operation, however, go at least four lbs. over these figures.

**A shock absorber** for the steering system runs from the front frame cross-member to the intermediate rod of the steering linkage. There's a stabilizer bar the width of the car running between the control arms. For front-end alignment camber and caster are adjusted through an eccentric cam in the upper control arm.

The carrying height of the Toronado

is regulated by adjusting a bolt on either of the front-end adjusting bars. Turning clockwise increases front-end height while a counterclockwise rotation decreases it.

Something quite new about this car is found in the drive axles. They are completely flexible and consist of an axle shaft on each side of the differential and an inner and outer constant-velocity joint. A torsional damper is mounted in the center of the right axle shaft. In disconnecting or removing the drive axles be extremely careful not to damage the joint seals.

The inner and outer joints are different and are designed to be replaced as a unit. They are disassembled only for repacking or replacing the seals.

Publicity on the Toronado has drawn a lot of attention to the enclosed chain connecting the torque converter to the input shaft of the gearbox. The chain is a link belt two in. wide and runs from a rubber-damped sprocket at the rear of the converter to a sprocket at the rear of the gearbox. The output spline shaft of the gearbox connects with the differential. If the link assembly is too long a sound like corn popping may be heard but beware—noise here also can result from worn or damaged engine mounts.

Toronado's crankcase ventilation system is of two varieties. The simpler one calls for replacing the valve annually, washing parts in kerosene and blowing out the hoses with compressed air. For the closed system it becomes necessary also to service the line between the valve cover and the carburetor. At every oil change wash the ventilation filter in kerosene and oil with SAE 10W-30 oil.

The cooling system, according to Olds, should contain ethylene-glycol antifreeze *all year round*. The company furthermore advises that the complete system should be drained and flushed every 24 months. Plain water is not recommended by Olds at any time!

Since the differential is up front it isn't likely to be as overlooked as looked over. Check the lube level at each oil change and fill to the level of the filler hole (capacity is 4½ pints). Be sure to clean around the plug before re-moving it. The steering linkage (tie rods and rod ends) should have a good multipurpose lubricant applied every 12 months or 12,000 mi. The ball joints are factory-lubricated for 36,000 mi. After that, inspect and lubricate them at 12,000-mi. intervals.

Actually, the trick lies not only in paying attention to what the Toronado *has* but also in considering what it *hasn't*. Don't bother looking for the drive shaft, for instance. There are universal joints (four) but they're between the differential and the front wheels.

The dead rear axle may seem too simple for attention but it has some important points to watch. The rear suspension, for example, can't be maintained unless the rear wheel bearings are adjusted correctly. These roller bearings are not repacked except when rear brake work is done. Then their cones must be a slip fit in the axle spindles. In order to permit the cones to creep you should lubricate them on the inside diameter. So important is the adjustment of these rear bearings that the wheel must be rotated while tightening the nut to 25 to 30 ft.-lbs. Then back off a half turn before inserting the cotter pin.

Toronado often is a surprise where you least expect it. Typical are the leaf springs for rear suspension. They're the single-leaf type with bushings front and rear. No clips—just center clamps with upper and lower insulators.

You can't start Toronado's engine by pushing the car. Use jumper wires to the battery, observing the rule about connections in parallel (positive to positive, negative to negative). It's not necessary to disconnect the alternator.

When jacking the car at the front, insert the lift pad into the 2½-in.-wide slot located about eight in. from the end of the bumper. At the rear the lift pad of the jack should straddle the bracket on the bumper's underside.

Towing preferably should be done with the front wheels off the ground but towing is permissible with the rear wheels raised if the transmission is in neutral, the speed doesn't exceed 45 mph and the distance is limited to 50 mi. •

AIR-FILTER replacement can improve an engine's power output dramatically.

# Easy Way to Get
# Ten Extra Horsepower

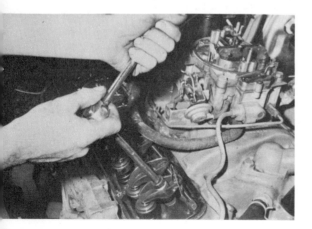

LIFTER ADJUSTMENT is recommended after tightening head bolts. Paper clip stops oil from squirting out of rocker feed holes.

WANT an extra 10 hp from your engine? No, you won't have to shave the cylinder heads or resort to expensive hot-rodding techniques. Chances are, you can pick up at least 10 hp—and often more—with these minor tuning jobs: replace the air filter, change the vacuum advance, wipe off the spark plugs, reroute ignition wires, adjust the timing, tighten the cylinder heads and adjust the valve lifters.

Each job will take two to 30 minutes and the whole list takes no more than two hours.

The simplest job is replacing the air filter. This can improve available horsepower dramatically, especially affecting acceleration and high-speed performance, as well as gas mileage and start-

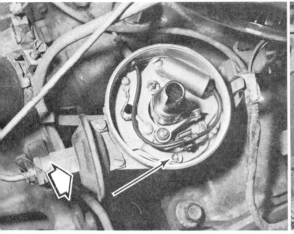

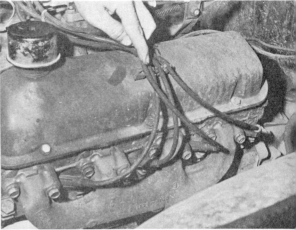

VACUUM-ADVANCE diaphragm is located in pie-plate housing (fat arrow). To remove, loosen screws and clip (slim arrow).

IGNITION-WIRE arrangement can cause or prevent crossfire. Wires going to plugs firing in sequence should be separated.

ing. On most cars, just unscrew the wing nut on the air-cleaner cover, pull out the dirty filter and install a new one.

If you have a filter made of polyurethane foam, you can clean it in solvent, dunk it in clean engine oil, squeeze out the excess and remount it on the metal frame. Easier still, replace it with a paper element made for your car. It's easier to service and needs service less frequently.

A clogged air filter can restrict air flow so badly that the engine is being

choked most of the time. It loses power, wastes gas and, in severe cases, makes starting difficult.

**If your car has over 35,000 mi.** on it or is four years old, replacing the distributor's vacuum advance unit should add several horsepower. The diaphragm in this unit advances the ignition timing at part throttle by shifting the position of the breaker point plate. As time goes by this diaphragm loses its airtightness and efficiency. The vacuum advance unit costs from $1.50 to $3 and on many

A TORQUE WRENCH is needed to tighten cylinder head bolts properly. This one reads to 150 ft.-lbs., costs about $10.

TIMING MARKS are way down low on the front of the engine. It's difficult and dangerous to align them with engine running.

cars it can be replaced without pulling out the distributor.

If the vacuum advance is in an awkward position, you can slacken the distributor lock and swing the distributor body into a more convenient position. But first paint a thin line along the distributor body and on the engine with nail polish or touchup paint. When you're finished, the mark will help align the distributor to maintain the timing settings.

The vacuum advance usually is screwed into the distributor body. The diaphragm has an actuating arm that connects to the breaker-point plate, generally by a clip. Just undo the clip, remove the mounting screws and disconnect the vacuum line from the carburetor base. The unit then will come right out.

**Merely wiping off the spark plugs** and checking the routing of the plug wires can eliminate many mysterious engine ailments.

Wiping off the plug terminals and insulators plus the metal clips on the ignition wires with a dry cloth prevents dirt and moisture from causing short circuits and voltage leaks.

Careful routing of the plug wires will prevent electromagnetic induction, commonly called crossfire. Crossfire can occur when two ignition wires run parallel and close to one another and the two plugs fire one right after the other. It is possible for the electrical impulse to be pulled from one wire to the other. The plug that should spark will fail, while the other one is firing away at the wrong time.

It is a particularly common problem on V8s because each bank has two cylinders that fire in sequence. The firing order will tell you which ones they are.

The thing to do is make sure that the wires to these two plugs are as far apart as possible or else cross each other at right angles. If there are plug wire guides built into the rocker cover, use them to keep the wires in place. If not, buy a set.

**Setting ignition timing accurately** can mean lots of extra horsepower. The typical weekend mechanic does the job either by ear or with a neon-tube timing light. Both have disadvantages. The timing light involves a tricky procedure that brings head and fingers perilously close to the spinning fan. Playing it by ear can cause engine damage if your ear is bad or the accessories drown out the critical sound you're listening for.

The easiest way to do the job is with the engine not running. The only tool is a test lamp. You can buy one for under $1 or make it from a 12-watt bulb. Merely solder one wire to the base of the bulb and another to the threaded side and attach alligator clips to the other ends of the wires.

First, a little theory: the spark has to be delivered to the plug when the piston is near the top of its stroke. The exact point is measured by the position of the crankshaft, using marks on the drive pulley or crank damper (at the front of the crankshaft) and a reference mark, usually a pointer, on the timing-chain cover. Lining up these marks means that the piston for the No. 1 cylinder is in the right position for the arrival of the spark. Once one cylinder is in time, all the others are.

In order to align these marks, we are going to crank over the engine with the starter until the marks are close to each other and finish the job by hand, using cars it can be replaced without pulling

SPARK PLUGS can collect dirt and moisture, causing voltage leaks and poor spark. Simply wipe clean with dry cloth.

the spark plugs first so you won't be fighting engine compression. It's also a good idea to remove the wire between the distributor cap and the coil so there is no juice flowing through the dangling ignition wires.

You will need the manufacturer's timing specs and if the pulley has several marks, you must find out what lines up with what. Auto-parts stores that serve professional mechanics have specification books and if you patronize them they'll look things like this up for you.

Once the marks are lined up, slacken the distributor lock so the distributor body can be rotated. Now connect one lead of the test lamp to the coil's thin wire terminal. It holds the wire that goes to the distributor body and should be marked CB, D, NEG or with a minus sign. Connect the other test-lamp wire to a metal part of the engine as ground. A cylinder-head bolt is fine.

Turn on the ignition and rotate the distributor body by hand through short arcs, first clockwise and then counterclockwise, until the bulb goes out. Once the bulb is out, slowly turn the distributor body in the opposite direction until it just starts to light. Then tighten the distributor lock.

What you have done is this: the test lamp will light when the points are open and go out when they're closed. You have to set the distributor so that the points are just opening, about to send a spark to No. 1 cylinder in a few thousandths of a second. And you know No. 1 cylinder is in the right position because the timing marks are lined up.

**The final jobs on the list,** tightening the head bolts and adjusting the valves, go together. When you tighten a cylinder head you reduce loss of compression from the cylinders (and loss of power). Two things are important: uniform tightening of the nuts or bolts and, where possible, readjustment of the valve lifters.

Uniform tightening requires a torque wrench, a tool that indicates—in foot-pounds—the amount of tightening force applied. For $10 you can get a torque wrench that will remain accurate for many years of weekend work. Get a 150-ft.-lb. model.

Head bolts are tightened in an imaginary spiral pattern from the center of the head outward to the ends. You will need the manufacturer's specifications as to the number of foot-pounds of tightening needed. Again, the auto-parts store is the place to go.

Once the head is tightened, the gasket is compressed and there is an effective change in the height of the engine. This changes valve timing a bit and, on cars with adjustable hydraulic valve lifters (Chevrolets and some Fords), you should readjust for maximum performance. Run the engine until fully warmed. Shut it down and pull the rocker cover (one at a time on V8s). You must prevent oil from squirting out of the feed holes in the rockers during idle. You can buy a set of oil stoppers for $3 or bend a large paper clip around the rocker and stick the end into the hole.

With the clips installed, run the engine at slow idle. Using a socket wrench, back off the adjusting nut in the center of the rocker (turn counterclockwise) until the valve just begins to clatter. Next, turn clockwise until the clatter just stops, which indicates that all clearance has been eliminated from the valve train.

Then turn the wrench an additional amount, specified by the manufacturer, to properly position the plunger and lifter. The specifications are given in full and half turns, such as 1½ turns. Check with that friendly parts store before you begin. In fact, be a sport. Buy the air cleaner, vacuum-advance unit and a set of points and plugs—and ask for the pile of specs all at once. Then keep a record of them.

Careful tuning may not bring a corpse back to life but it can add a nice touch of liveliness to a car that just needs a tonic.

If you follow our procedure carefully you'll find our extra-10-hp is a conservative figure. If you don't pick up two or more times that amount of power there probably will be a reason—you've been taking good care of your car all along. •

# GIVE YOUR CAR A $40 PAINT JOB!

STAN is a rugged, sandy-haired man whose big hands are rough from years of auto-body work. We were almost afraid to tell him we were planning to paint a car ourselves—we expected him to laugh or at least try to discourage us. He did neither.

"A few years ago I'd have told you to forget it," Stan said, "but with the new fast-drying paints on the market anybody can do a good job." He paused and added, "If he's careful, that is."

Stan is an old friend who has hammered out many a wrinkled fender. He sat down with us for a half hour, outlined all the necessary steps and listed $40 worth of materials we would need. These included one gallon of acrylic lacquer, one gallon of Acry-Seal sealer-primer, two gallons of lacquer thinner, one gallon of degreaser and solvent, four paint strainers, a spraying mask, two rolls of masking tape, a small can of body putty, a tack cloth, a rubber squeegee, a dozen sheets each of Nos. 220, 320, 400 and 600 sandpaper, three sheets of No. 180 sandpaper, six coarse sanding disks, a tube of sanding-disk adhesive and a week's savings of newspapers and rags. A week later the worn and scuffed Austin-Healey shone like new.

The Austin-Healey is a relatively small sports roadster. If you are painting a large American sedan you will need more paint, lacquer thinner and possibly sandpaper but the rest of the quantities listed should be sufficient.

*Here's how it's done.*

Before starting the job, get all body damage (dents, tears and holes) re-

40

REMOVE as much chrome trim as possible. This eliminates masking and exposes rust.

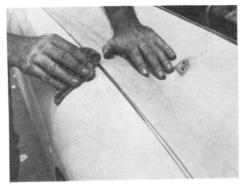

WIPE off entire car with a rag liberally doused in degreaser solvent to cut road tar.

GRIND all rust spots down to bare metal. A sanding disk is best for contoured areas.

SAND entire body, using plenty of water and a squeegee to check for missed spots.

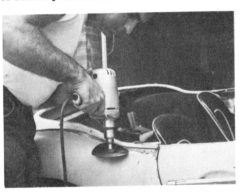

paired. You can do this yourself with one of the inexpensive fiberglass repair kits on the market. Don't worry about minor dimples and rust spots until later.

Remove every part that is not to be painted (side trim, headlight rims, taillights, door molding, grille, handles, mirrors, bumpers, etc.). We removed the hood and trunk lid to work around the edges more easily but this isn't always necessary.

Dechroming takes only a couple of hours if you're lucky but a few frozen hard-to-reach nuts could make it an all-day operation. One hint that will save you time later: keep nuts and bolts and small hardware from each component together in labeled envelopes.

If your old paint is so bad it must be removed, buy a can of non-alkaline paint remover. Spread it on with a large, well-

worn brush and wipe away the paint. Repeat as necessary until most of the paint has been removed.

If the old paint isn't too bad, go on and remove grease, dirt and wax from the body with the degreaser and solvent. This step also is necessary after using paint remover to take off the waxy residue. Pour the degreasing liquid liberally on a clean rag and rub the body briskly. This must be done before sanding the old paint to avoid driving the grime deeper into the finish. From here on avoid touching the car with your hands —the oil in your skin could keep the new paint from sticking.

**Do the roughest sanding first.** Rust spots (often found below doors and around side trim) must be ground down to bare, shiny metal with a coarse sanding disk or grinding wheel. If you don't

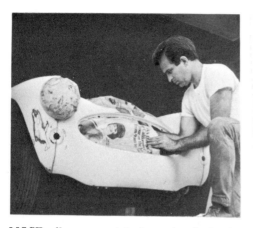 

MASK all areas not to be painted. Apply primer and sand again, repeat as necessary.

AFTER painting, allow an overnight drying period, then polish with rubbing compound.

own an electric drill or grinder, borrow or rent one. You'll need it for only a few minutes, but it will save you hours of hand-sanding.

After grinding, sand the area with No. 220 sandpaper until the circular grinding marks are gone.

Now sand the entire body, first with No. 220, then No. 320 and finally No. 400 sandpaper. Don't use a sanding block—it reduces the contact area. Dip the sandpaper frequently in a pail of water as you work to clear residue from the grit and to lubricate the work. Wiping the water from the sanded area with a rubber squeegee will help you see spots you may have missed. Sand in long, horizontal strokes; never cross-sand.

Tiny nicks in the old paint can be feather-edged by applying pressure behind the sandpaper with a single fingertip. When you have finished, the entire body should be covered with barely noticeable lines resembling fine record grooves. *If your fingers should touch the body during sanding, apply degreaser to the spot immediately.*

After sanding, wash the entire body with warm water and a lint-free rag, wipe with more clean rags and allow to dry for several hours, preferably overnight.

Next, mask off all areas not to be painted, such as headlights, window glass, tires and grille opening. Apply

masking tape along the edge of a newspaper and press carefully along the edge of the area to be covered. In hard-to-reach places first apply tape alone and then tape-edged newspaper.

**Before spraying,** hose down the garage floor and sweep out the dust. Most paint-spraying failures result from dust. A garage is essential—don't try to spray outdoors. One veteran body man hangs a chain from a bumper bracket to the floor to ground the car and prevent static electricity from attracting dust. Whether this works is debatable but it certainly can't hurt.

If you don't own a compressor and spray gun, you can rent one from a paint store for a few dollars a day. Be sure to get a gun with an external-mix nozzle, one that mixes the paint and air on the outside. Lacquer tends to clog an internal-mix nozzle.

Stir in one and a half parts of lacquer thinner to one part Acry-Seal primer-sealer and practice your spraying on some scrap cardboard. Before starting on the car, wipe the body with a tack cloth, a rag lightly dampened with solvent that picks up dust.

For large panels, adjust the gun to deliver a fan-shaped pattern about two or three in. high and eight or ten in. wide. For tight areas such as wheels and door edges use a small, round pattern the size of a silver dollar. As you spray from six to ten in. away, the primer-sealer should go on wet but not so wet that it runs. A spraying mask may feel hot and uncomfortable but it will keep a lot of pigment out of your lungs.

As you move the gun from side to side, always keep it the same distance from the work. Keep the nozzle always perpendicular to the car surface. Don't swing the gun in an arc. And always keep the gun moving. First start your stroke, then press the trigger. After you release the trigger, follow through with the stroke past the edge of the working area.

Spray in horizontal strokes from the top down to avoid brushing against a freshly sprayed area while reaching across the body. Overlap your strokes by a third or more to avoid streaks and unpainted areas.

Allow the car to dry for a half hour, then search for dimples or low spots where you feathered the paint. Level such spots with body putty applied with a squeegee. If the low spots are deep, apply a thin layer of putty, allow to dry for a half hour and cover with another thin layer. Let the putty dry for at least four hours, then *dry sand* with Nos. 180, 220, 320 and 400 sandpaper. Using water at this stage would hurt paint adhesion. Since the putty is softer than steel, use a sanding block to get a smooth surface. Wipe away sanding dust with the tack cloth, reprime the repaired areas and wait another half hour.

Though you can paint over Acry-Seal without sanding first, it is a good idea to go over the entire car lightly with dry No. 400 sandpaper.

Finally you are ready to spray on the paint. By now you should feel more at ease with the spray gun. The priming operation wasn't critical since mistakes are easy to sand down and respray. But with paint, repairs are more difficult.

Stir the paint thoroughly (a piece of coat-hanger wire bent into a squared-off hook and chucked in a power drill makes the job easier). Then filter the paint through a strainer to remove lumps and mix it with an equal volume of lacquer thinner. If you decide not to use acrylic lacquer, check the instructions on the paint can for the proper thinning ratio. Or, check with your paint supplier. Follow his advice to prevent mistakes.

Go over the car once again with a tack cloth and, using the same technique as in priming, apply four or five coats to the entire car. There's no need to wait between coats—by the time you finish one end of the car the other will be dry and ready for more paint.

Wet-sand the entire car lightly with No. 600 sandpaper, wipe thoroughly with clean rags and allow to dry several hours, preferably overnight. Then wipe with a tack cloth and spray on four or five lighter paint coats, using one and a half parts thinner to one part paint. Start with heavy coats and finish with light ones to obtain a finish with maximum gloss.

The next day you can polish the surface with rubbing compound and reinstall the trim and accessories. But wait at least two months before waxing to make sure no moisture is trapped in the paint. •

PROBE badly rusted areas with screwdriver. If the metal gives, first get the area repaired.

TRUNK and hood lids can be removed for sanding and spraying if the edges are rusty.

43

# What you can (and can't) do to your
# AUTO AIR CONDITIONER

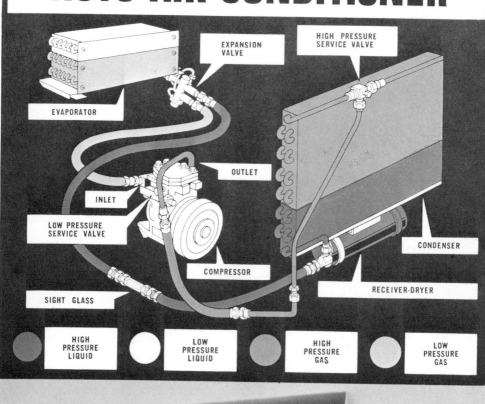

EXPANSION VALVE

HIGH PRESSURE SERVICE VALVE

EVAPORATOR

OUTLET

INLET

LOW PRESSURE SERVICE VALVE

COMPRESSOR

CONDENSER

SIGHT GLASS

RECEIVER-DRYER

HIGH PRESSURE LIQUID

LOW PRESSURE LIQUID

HIGH PRESSURE GAS

LOW PRESSURE GAS

OBTAINING top performance from your auto's air conditioner requires a bit more than driving into a service shop once a year for a $15 refrigerant recharge. Now don't wince at the thought of your laboring over a mass of intricate air conditioning components—we said a *bit more*, didn't we?

Actually, to check out your A/C system, you need only your hands, eyes, a thermometer and about an hour's spare time. That's right—no special tools, no

---

### HOW THEY WORK

The compressor changes Freon to a hot gas by increasing its pressure. The condenser is exposed to cool air flow and changes the hot gas to a cool but not cold liquid. The receiver/dryer removes any moisture and stores excess Freon. The expansion valve passes a small amount of liquid to the evaporator.

At this point, the gas pressure drops sharply (due to the suction of the compressor) and causes the liquid to change back into a gas. However, in the process of changing from liquid to gas, the refrigerant draws heat from the evaporator, which, in turn, draws off heat from the passenger compartment and cools it.

---

gauges, not even a wrench is necessary.

In fact, as Freon is a somewhat hazardous gas, under no circumstances should you ever disconnect any unit or hose containing Freon. Nor should you attempt to add more refrigerant. If the following tests show that the system does need some Freon, have it done by an air conditioning specialist.

**The cooling source** is the compressor, so first make certain there is no slippage between the drive belt and the compressor pulley. (Note that the compressor pulley rotates at all times. When the A/C power switch is turned to On, a magnetic clutch connects the drive pulley to the compressor shaft.)

Since you probably don't have a tension or torsion gauge to check the belt tension, just press down on the belt be-

tween the compressor pulley and the engine's damper pulley. If the belt moves no more than $1/4$ to $3/8$ inch, you can be sure there is no slippage. Be certain to make this check when the belt is *hot* from running. If you have the car's A/C manual, check for the amount of play specified.

Turn the A/C to On and let it run for 15 to 20 minutes. Then place your hand on the hose from the compressor output (where it enters the condenser) and note how hot it feels. Move your hand to the condenser's output hose (generally at the top). It should feel somewhat cooler than the input hose—still hot, but not as hot as the input hose. If the temperatures seem about the same, the condenser isn't cooling the gas properly. The trouble may be caused by dirt clogging the condenser fins, so as a matter of course, clean the condenser every year by scrubbing it vigorously with a stiff brush. Then use a shop vacuum to alternately blow and suck the loosened dirt from the condenser.

**Move on to the receiver/dryer** and check for clogging by placing your hand on the input hose (the one coming from the condenser) and then the output

COMPRESSOR drive belt must be tight and free of grease to insure good efficiency.

hose (the one going to the expansion valve). Both hoses should feel *equal* in temperature. A clogged filter is generally indicated by an output hose cooler than the input hose. Sorry, but a clogged receiver requires a service shop repair. *Don't try to do it yourself.*

Check the hose at the input to the expansion valve. This usually is located at the firewall in the engine compartment on factory A/Cs or at the evaporator input of add-on models. The hose input to the valve should be hot—if you can feel or get to the valve's output it should be cold. If the hose going in feels cool or if it's hot coming out, your next stop is the service shop.

The output hose from the evaporator to the compressor should be cold. On a cool day you'll even see frost on the metal hose fittings right at the compressor. If the output hose is only *cool*, and not cold, the expansion valve may be ready for replacement or adjustment.

**After the initial check-up**, belt tightening and condenser cleaning, set the car in the sun with the windows closed and allow the A/C to run for about a half hour. Then check the sight glass (usually part of the receiver or condenser.) If you see bubbles in the sightglass, the A/C needs additional refrigerant. Note that the bubble check is made *during* operation. It's normal to see bubbles for several minutes after the A/C is turned off.

Next check the cooling efficiency. If yours is a factory installation the car's service manual generally will list the temperature differential that should be measured. An add-on unit generally is rated to drop the inside temperature 15° below the outside air temperature. (Thus if it's 100° outside it's not going to be cooler than 85° inside the car.) If you don't have this information in your factory installation use the 15° test. Position a thermometer over the back of the front seat at about eye level and check that the temperature at this point is 15° below the outside temperature. If you measure less than 15° you might need more refrigerent or a new expansion valve. Have the system checked by an auto A/C *specialist.*

Since air conditioners remove water

A DIRTY radiator will reduce efficiency. Clean with a stiff wire brush and vacuum.

RADIATOR must contain anti-freeze rated at 15° or lower. Check with a hydrometer.

RECEIVER/DRYER isn't clogged if input and output hoses are at same temperature.

(moisture) from the air, make certain the drain holes are open. Otherwise you're likely to get a lap full of water or a block of ice in the evaporator. Add-on models have rubber drain hoses running through holes in the floor. Simply pull up the hoses and check that they aren't clogged with road dirt (which is easily accumulated during the winter months). A few wiggles with a straightened section of coathanger is all it takes to clean the drains. The drain holes for factory installations usually are on, or under, the firewall outside the passenger compartment.

Since the cooling of the condenser is dependent upon sufficient air flow through the condenser and radiator, make certain the radiator is clean. If cleaning is necessary, use a stiff brush and a vacuum. But be careful not to bend and damage the soft metal fins of the radiator. This would prevent cooling air from passing through.

It also is important to have the car's regular cooling system at top efficiency —a hot radiator or engine will reduce the amount of condenser cooling considerably. Make certain the thermostat is working and that the radiator pressure cap is holding at the rated pressure. Also make certain the radiator cap has the correct pressure rating. Cars with factory A/Cs use a cap with a higher pressure rating—never replace it with a standard pressure cap.

**Electrical woes** are not to be overlooked, either. The extra load of the compressor's electric clutch and the evaporator fan can be as high as 17 amperes.

Thus, factory installed A/Cs usually come as a package with a heavy duty alternator capable of handling the extra current requirements. On the other hand, with an add-on A/C you're stuck with the original generator or alternator—in which case it's possible to exhaust its current handling capacity to the point where there isn't enough juice left to charge a rundown battery. Since just a slight decrease in electrical efficiency can mean insufficient charging current to handle the ignition, A/C and lights, make certain you get all the current the generator or alternator can deliver. Check the generator or alternator belt for excessive play—about ¼ to ⅜ inch in each direction is normal.

With a battery known to be fully charged, check that the combined A/C and bright light current drain does not cause the idiot light or ammeter to show a discharge. If you do get a discharge indication have the voltage regulator checked.

If you have an add-on unit and the car radio is a tube model, the combined drain of the ignition, A/C, brights *and* radio may prove just too much for the charging system—and the charge indicator always will show discharge. One solution is to shut off the radio when the A/C is on. Another is to install a heavy duty generator or alternator. If your car is equipped with a generator that can handle the extra current, you might instead try using an adjustable regulator (one with a knob adjustment that increases the amount of charging current). You can set the regulator to provide extra current needed.

**The added load** of the A/C compressor on the engine will cause the normal idle speed to decrease. On six cylinder engines the decrease will be 50 to 100 rpm, enough to cause the engine to idle roughly or stall. Simply increase the hot idle adjustment (when the A/C is on) to the rated rpm. If you don't have a tachometer and don't feel like paying a mechanic for a two-second adjustment, simply turn the idle screw very slowly until the roughness just disappears— this will usually restore engine performance. Don't forget to slow the idle speed back to normal come fall.

If your A/C is an add-on model your spring check-up is finished. But if it's a factory job you've got one more step. Most factory installations have the evaporator mounted next to the heater core. Since no heater water is circulated during the summer, the evaporator can freeze the water in the heater—resulting in a ruptured or burst heater. *So never remove the antifreeze from a car with a factory A/C.* In fact, check that the anti-freeze protection during the A/C months is to 15° or lower. •

# Taking Care of an Air-Cooled Engine

CORVAIR ENGINE, like other air-cooled models, is enclosed in sheet-metal shrouding (above). A fan forces air between shroud and finned cylinders. The fan belt (below) follows a tortuous route. Guides installed in 1962 keep belt on the pulleys.

A CAR radiator can be a pain. It needs to be drained and flushed twice a year. When the temperature dips, it demands antifreeze. Sometimes it clogs or leaks, or its hoses pinch or split, leaving you at the roadside with your hood up and your spirits down.

The obvious answer to these annoyances is to buy a car without a radiator —one that is air-cooled. You can choose from the American-made Chevrolet Corvair; the German Volkswagen, Porsche and NSU; the French Citroen AMI-6 and 2 CV; and the Dutch Daf 44 and Daffodil.

But keep in mind that an air-cooling system isn't completely trouble-free, no matter what the ads imply. Maintenance

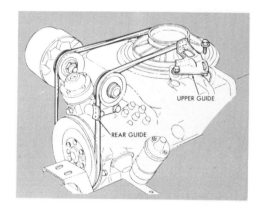

and repair are easier in some ways, tougher in others. And many service procedures are entirely different from those required by water-cooled engines.

Most motorcycle and aircraft engines need no cooling system since they are entirely exposed to the airstream. An air-cooled car engine, on the other hand, is enclosed by body panels; air must be forced mechanically past its cylinder and head surfaces to carry away combustion heat. This is done with an engine-powered blower fan, which draws air from the engine compartment and pushes it through sheet-metal shrouding bolted all around the engine. The cylinder and head surfaces underneath the shrouding are finned for better heat dissipation.

**In the Volkswagen 1600,** Citroen, NSU, and Daf, the fan is mounted next to the engine and runs directly off the crankshaft. In the Corvair, Volkswagen Beetle, and Porsche, the blower is mounted on top of the engine for the sake of compactness and is powered by a belt.

In time the belt stretches and slips, causing engine overheating. The Porsches and 140-hp. (four-carburetor) Corvairs have temperature gauges, and other cars have dashboard warning lights, but by the time any overheating from belt slippage shows up on these instruments, the belt may be badly damaged. To avoid this, check belt tension regularly (at least every 6,000 miles). With a new belt, make your first check within 300 miles. In fact, the Corvair manual suggests running-in a new belt at 1,500 rpm for at least two minutes and rechecking the tension. And Porsche recommends several checks during the first 100 miles.

**Belt adjustment in most cars** isn't too critical. The Volkswagen manual, for example, says only that under moderate finger pressure the belt should deflect about 0.6 in. Porsche gives a leeway of 0.5 to 0.75 in.

The Corvair manual, however, is stricter; it insists that a strand tension gauge be used, with a new belt tensioned to 70-80 lbs. The reason is that the Corvair belt undergoes two 90° twists, making it hard to find a straight surface for a deflection check. Although a brand new Corvair belt should be tensioned to 70-80 lbs., one that's run a few hundred miles should be tensioned to only 50-60 lbs. If you were to frequently readjust the belt to 70 or 80 lbs., you would be inviting failure. An overtight belt in any car may break or may damage generator and alternator bearings.

**Some slack in the belt** can be taken up in the Corvair by loosening the bolts holding the idler-pulley bracket (on the right side of the engine) and prying the bracket with a bar.

The Volkswagen Beetle and the Porsches use a V-groove generator pulley consisting of two halves separated by spacer washers. Removing washers brings the pulley halves together, forcing the belt higher in the groove and increasing tension. To keep from losing the removed washers, slip them onto the generator shaft between the outer pulley half and retaining nut. When the belt is stretched to a point where no washers remain between the pulley halves, you need a new belt.

In 1960 and 1961, the first years of the Corvair's introduction, owners were plagued by thrown belts resulting from rollover. Since then the belt has been rounded along the bottom corners to improve pulley entry, and changes in the outer wrapping material allow it to slip slightly under sudden load, such as during a downshift. Belt guides have been mounted on the idler and blower pulleys to help keep the belt in place. If you own one of the early Corvairs, you can adapt these guides to your car.

**But what do you do if** a belt breaks on the road and you don't have a spare? With most cars you stop and wait for help. The Corvair, however, can keep going until the battery runs down because of the inoperative alternator. The Corvair's separate electric heater blower can pull enough air through the engine to provide some cooling. If you keep speed down to 15 or 20 mph—just fast enough to stay in high gear—and switch on the blower, turn on the heat, and open a couple of windows to reduce air-flow restriction, you can safely limp to the nearest garage. If the temperature-warning light goes on, stop and

**VOLKSWAGEN has a belt pulley made in two halves with washers in between. Removing washers forces the belt higher in the groove and tightens it. Washers are stored on shaft.**

turn off the engine, leaving the heater blower (and heat) turned on. When the light goes out, it's safe to drive on.

Sometimes, after a hard run uphill or at high speed with a trailer, the engine may overheat even with the belt intact. Reducing speed usually brings engine temperature down quickly.

The Citroens have no auxiliary heater blower and turning on the heater has no effect on engine temperature. In some other air-cooled cars, turning on the heater diverts part of the air away from the cylinder surfaces, resulting in worse overheating.

**For faster engine warmup,** some air-cooled cars use a thermostat that decreases the air flow to or from the engine blower until the engine reaches operating temperature.

In earlier Volkswagens the thermostat actuated a doughnut-shaped throttle ring that tilted to admit more air to the blower. In recent models these rings are replaced by flaps at the exhaust end of the engine shrouding. In case of thermostat failure, the flaps are spring-loaded to open, to provide adequate cooling at all times. Of course this situation would result in much slower engine warmup. In cold weather the engine might not ever warm up properly. And unfortunately, the flaps are underneath the engine, where they can't be seen readily.

The VW has no temperature gauge so, to check whether the thermostat is functioning, you have to reach into the engine compartment in front of the shroud and feel the position of the connecting link between the left and right flaps. When the link is all the way to the right, the flaps are fully open. When the engine is cold, the link should be in the left position, with flaps partly closed. Otherwise, the only clue to a malfunctioning thermostat is sluggish performance and poor gas mileage.

The 1960 Corvair used a thermostat-operated ring something like the Volkswagen's. In later models, however, the thermostat operates two flaps that close off the grille opening below the rear bumper, forcing blower air to recirculate through the engine. These flaps are visible from behind the car, and are easy to check.

**Removing the Corvair thermostat** is more difficult than in a water-cooled car, but it's nothing a do-it-yourselfer can't handle. The rear end must be raised and the bottom shroud removed; the thermostat is integral with this panel. Once the thermostat has been replaced, the adjusting rod must be set so that when it is pulled out as far as it goes, the grille flap is fully open. To do this, you must temporarily attach the bottom shrouding with two bolts (one to the crankcase, one to the cylinder head).

When you get the proper setting, remove the shrouding, connect the retaining clip on the adjusting rod and reinstall the shrouding.

In the Volkswagen Beetle the thermostat can be reached from under the right side of the engine without removing any shrouding. Before raising the car on a lift, reach into the engine compartment and push the connecting link for the air flaps all the way to the right to open the flaps. The thermostat bracket has slots to allow adjustment. Set the bracket so that the thermostat touches the upper part of the bracket. Then tighten the two bracket nuts.

**The Porsche, NSU, Citroen and Daf** have no blower thermostat, nor have they an automatic means of varying air flow to the engine. The Daf and Citroen do, however, provide blocking plates that are manually slipped behind the grille at the start of winter to partially block air flow to the blower.

The blower itself doesn't normally require service in any air-cooled car. There have been cases of leaves being sucked in and clogging the blades, but this is rare.

Since air-cooled engines run substantially hotter than do their water-cooled counterparts, most use an oil cooler to keep engine oil from thinning out excessively and losing its lubricating properties. This is nothing more than a miniature finned radiator inside the engine shrouding, through which the oil passes. NSU is the only manufacturer that doesn't install an oil cooler in all their cars; they feel it's necessary only on their TTS model, which is designed for racing and rallying.

These oil coolers rarely require maintenance. Only the Corvair shop manual suggests brushing accumulated dirt out of the oil-cooler fins every 12,000 miles (this can be done by removing a cover plate).

For the sake of maintaining reasonably even temperature distribution along the engine walls, air-cooled engines use unit-cylinder construction, with each individual cylinder secured by four studs. This design allows cooling air to sweep entirely around each cylinder, picking up heat from its fins. Because of this design requirement, the motorist benefits in several ways. As one cylinder at a time can be replaced, there is no need to scrap the entire engine if you throw a rod. All the cylinders can be replaced instead of re-boring the block.

**Another servicing advantage** of air-cooling is that the higher cylinder temperatures allow cleaner burning of fuel, slowing down the formation of carbon deposits.

A big air-cooling minus, however, is poor engine accessibility. For all but the simplest maintenance jobs the blower and shrouding get in the way. On some engines you can't even see the spark plugs. And in engines having two banks of cylinders you have to separate the crankcase halves for any work on the lower end—which means pulling the engine. In all fairness, though, the smaller engines are easy to remove and replace (Volkswagen's conservative estimate is an hour and a quarter in and out).

**One odd thing about the Volkswagen** line: apparently the No. 3 cylinder tends to run hotter than the others. To make up for this, the distributor cam is set so the timing on that cylinder is retarded two degrees. This means that you can't time the engine on that cylinder. Use cylinder No. 1.

The heater is another sore spot in air-cooled designs. Heat is picked up either from the engine surfaces or from exhaust-pipe heat exchanger. Neither method is as effective as a water heater, especially at low speeds and under stop-and-go conditions. Supplementary gas-burning heaters are standard on some Porsches and optional on many other air-cooled cars; these do the job, but at the expense of fuel economy.

Whatever make of air-cooled car you drive, be sure to keep the engine clean. Unpleasant odors from an oil stain on a hot engine shroud could be sucked into the passenger compartment by the blower when you turn on the heater.

But if you'd rather spend your weekends at the golf course or in the hammock instead of flushing a radiator or replacing water hoses, air is answer. •

# 10-Point Checklist For

NEARLY any weekend mechanic can work up a lot of enthusiasm for a tune up of his car—even a relatively major amount of adjusting—but when it comes to the host of quick, simple and unglamorous jobs that, with a modest amount of effort, can contribute so much to a car's health—the average car enthusiast would rather be doing something else.

Yet an overwhelming majority of the cars on the road at any given time are badly in need of just such minor work. The ten little jobs illustrated here by no means exhaust the list but they are important and, when completed, have results any driver can notice.

You might call them Tom Tappett's Top Ten, though you probably could add another ten yourself. The point is that, once you have started doing this kind of minor maintenance work on your car, you are likely to be so enthusiastic with the results that you will go on to other areas which also will yield much satisfaction with only a little labor.

For example, on the battery—straight ammonia is a better cleaner than the time-honored baking-soda solution and easier to use. But don't get any into the battery because it will dilute the acid, as will baking soda. While you're at it, tighten the battery cables and grease the terminals.

When you clean the inlet breather make sure you wipe up all excess oil, which is bound to flow downwards, especially after the engine becomes warm. Horsehair filters should be cleaned but not oiled; pleated paper ones are simply replaced.

Do your wife a favor if she ever has to change a flat. Prevent the lug nuts from rusting on tight by removing them, wire-brushing the studs with kerosene and giving them a light coat of grease.

It always is a good idea to take a look at the *bottom* of your car. Check the

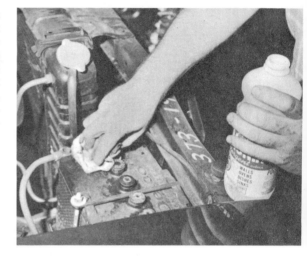

1. CLEAN OFF THE TOP of your battery from time to time with household ammonia and a rag. This removes accumulated oil, dirt and corrosion, which can bleed off power and eat away hold-down brackets.

2. WIPE OFF HEADLAMPS and other lights with ammonia and water mixture. Road film dulls headlamps and virtually impregnates itself into plastic lenses, cutting down your ability to see and be seen at night.

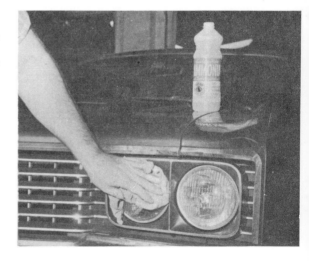

# Backyard Mechanics

3. SOAK THE INLET BREATHER in kerosene or some other common solvent. The breather, usually built into the oil-filler cap, is often neglected even by professional mechanics. Oil wire mesh filters after cleaning them.

5. SPRAY RUBBER MOLDING around fender skirts with a silicon lubricant or brake fluid to keep it from gluing itself to the bodywork. This is just one of many jobs that make changing a flat easier for the wife and you.

4. LUBRICATE THE SPEEDOMETER CABLE with a handy product called speedometer grease. This is a once-a-year job that should prevent speedo trouble forever. Use the grease on door, hood and deck lid hinges too.

6. INSPECT THE EXHAUST SYSTEM the next time the chassis is lubricated. Bang it around pretty well to make sure the hangers are in good shape. If they give out on the road you can lose the entire exhaust system.

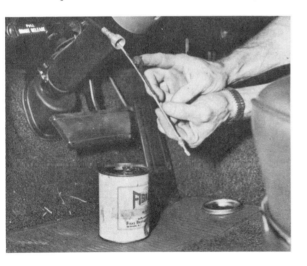

**7. SPRAY THE CARBURETOR LINKAGE** at least twice a year with an aerosol carb cleaner to remove oil and dirt. Never oil the linkage—it creates a sticky surface that will attract dirt even faster than usual.

**9. REMOVE THE LEAVES** that accumulate behind the grill and on the radiator in the fall. Gravity won't do this job because road film and squashed bugs make a good adhesive. A bad case can cause overheating.

**8. REGLUE PARTIALLY LOOSENED** weather stripping as soon as you notice it. If you let it go for too long, the rubber can become badly misshapen or get chopped up in the door itself. Then it's a big job.

**10. CHECK YOUR BRAKE SYSTEM** visually by removing the reservoir cover and looking for dirt or obvious discoloration. Next, get inside the car and check the pedal feel for sponginess and excess travel.

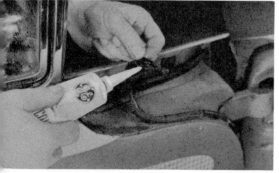

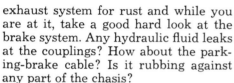

exhaust system for rust and while you are at it, take a good hard look at the brake system. Any hydraulic fluid leaks at the couplings? How about the parking-brake cable? Is it rubbing against any part of the chasis?

One important part of the car which should never be overlooked is the brake fluid reservoir. If it's a new car, check *both* brake fluid reservoirs. When filling the reservoir, if at all possible, always use the same brand of hydraulic brake fluid. While mixing brands is permissible, it is possible for one brand to froth when mixed with another. Make sure the fluid is marked SAE 70-R3.

You should have at least an inch of clearance between the brake pedal and the floor board when you step down hard on the brake. Keep your foot on the brake for at least a minute to make certain that the pedal does not travel farther. If it does, have the system inspected. ●

# Give your
# CAR A $10 PHYSICAL

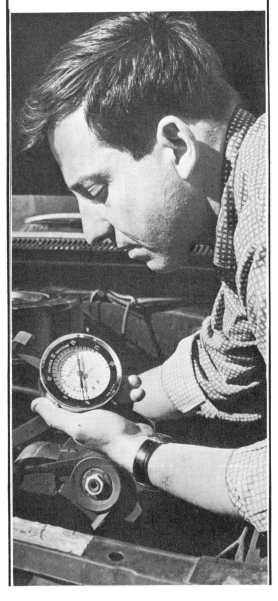

CONNECTING a vacuum gauge to your car's intake manifold is like telling the engine to open wide and say a-a-ah. This deceptively simple-looking gauge sells for under $10 yet often can tell you more than elaborate service-station equipment costing hundreds of dollars.

Essentially, a vacuum gauge checks out your engine's breathing—the way it draws in fuel and air and expels burned gases. Since most engine ailments—whether intake, exhaust or ignition—have a marked effect on manifold vacuum, a vacuum gauge can spot trouble well before performance falls off noticeably. What's more, it can help pinpoint the source of trouble with amazing accuracy.

Some of the conditions it will spot are intake leak; balky spark plug; carburetor out of adjustment; clogged exhaust; wrong ignition timing; piston blowby; improper spark-plug gap; blown head gasket; sticky, burned or leaky valve; incorrect valve timing; weak or broken valve spring; maladjusted or pitted distributor points and bad condenser. An impressive list, you must admit.

Even if you don't do your own mechanical repairs, the vacuum gauge is a great di-

# CAR CARE

agnostic aid. Use it to make sure your friendly neighborhood garage doesn't sell you a complete valve job when all you need is distributor points.

**For all the tests** outlined here, a portable vacuum gauge is handiest. It permits you to take a reading right at the engine and make simultaneous adjustments single-handedly. However, you also may wish to mount a vacuum gauge permanently on the dash.

One advantage of a permanent gauge is that you can spot trouble through changes in readings under similar driving conditions. When you drive the same car from day to day it's almost impossible to detect gradual loss of tune by feel alone.

Installation of a vacuum gauge is exceptionally easy in older cars with vacuum-operated windshield wipers. Pull the wiper hose from the manifold fitting and slip on the vacuum-gauge hose. Some cars not equipped with vacuum wipers have a tapped hole in the intake manifold sealed with a 1/8-in. pipe-thread plug. Replace this plug with an appropriate fitting and connect the gauge.

However, in many cars, you must drill and tap the intake manifold yourself. No need to remove the manifold. To catch chips, grease the drill bit liberally and back it out often. On cars with dual carburetors without a balance pipe, drill two holes, one at each intake port, and bridge them with rubber tubing and a tee fitting.

**Let's put the gauge** to work. Before starting the tests, warm up the engine thoroughly. Then check the reading on the gauge while the engine is idling. At sea level a healthy engine should give a steady reading between 17 and 22 in. At altitudes above 2,000 ft., readings drop about one in. every 1,000 ft. While several other variables can affect readings, bear in mind that numerical values are less significant than the action of the pointer.

If your car is an older model your first test should be of compression. The

best method is to let the engine idle, then open and close the throttle quickly. The pointer should drop to well below five in., rebound to about 25, then settle down to a normal idle reading.

The reason is this: as the throttle opens abruptly, a large supply of air is introduced quickly into the manifold. But the piston speed takes a while to

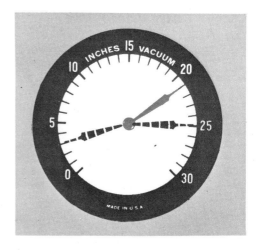

CHECK compression by idling engine, then opening and closing throttle rapidly. Pointer should drop to near zero, swing up slightly past normal, then settle back to normal.

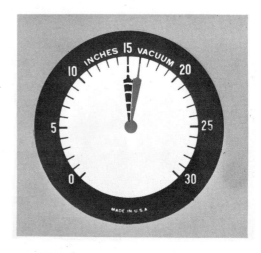

A READING slightly below normal with a periodic drop of one in. indicates plugs are gapped incorrectly or points are bad. This is more noticeable on a V-4 than a V-8.

increase and to pump up vacuum. Similarly, when the throttle is closed, air flow into the manifold is cut off abruptly but the piston speed goes down only gradually. The amount and rapidity of kickback on the gauge from open to closed throttle gives a good indication of engine compression. If the pointer rebounds to below 22 as you open and close the throttle, suspect worn rings. If the pointer drops to near zero slowly and then just creeps back to normal or slightly higher, the engine probably is in generally bad condition.

**A steady reading** below normal at idle indicates either an intake leak or retarded ignition timing. A blown carburetor or manifold gasket, or a hole

STEADY reading below normal indicate intake leak or retarded timing. Since leaks are more noticeable at idle, suspect the timing if reading drops drastically at high rpm.

FLOATING pointer 3 or 4 in. below normal indicates a rich carburetor mixture. Check the inside of exhaust pipe: gray coating is normal, black coating means rich mixture.

OCCASIONAL drop of about four in. is due to sticky valve. Each time it sticks it breaks vacuum. Few drops of penetrating oil in each guide frees and identifies bad valve.

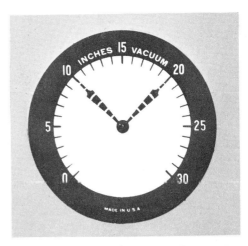

VIBRATING reading on gauge will result if valve springs are weak. This will not show up at idle or low engine speeds so be certain to run this test at a high rpm.

in the manifold or carburetor body, can cause loss of vacuum. To find the leak, use a section of old garden hose as a stethoscope and listen for the telltale hiss. You also can check visually by squirting oil around the suspected area, then watching for bubbles.

Slight adjustments to ignition timing can be made with the vernier adjustment near the base of the distributor. If the timing is way off, though, loosen the lock nut at the base of the distributor and turn the housing. Adjust for the highest steady gauge reading, then retard the timing until the gauge shows a one-in. drop.

A fluctuating pointer in the normal range (about 17 to 22) means advanced timing. Again adjust the distributor for the highest steady reading, then back off one in. on the gauge.

If the reading is exceptionally low and steady and adjustment of ignition timing doesn't help, suspect late valve timing. If it's only slightly late the gauge probably won't show it. But your dash temperature gauge will—the engine will overheat.

**A sharp rhythmic drop** of up to 10 in. from a normal reading while the engine is idling indicates a leak in the area of the cylinder head. You often can feel the leak from a blown head gasket with your hand unless the blowout is between two cylinders inside the engine. In the latter case, the needle may show an even greater rhythmic drop. Other possibilities are a head that is torqued improperly or warped. If retorquing to manufacturer's specifications doesn't help, replace the gasket. If this still doesn't remedy the condition, have the heads milled.

A pointer floating with a slow, regular movement between about 13 and 16 in. indicates an overrich mixture. This may be due to clogged carburetor air cleaner, sticking carburetor float or improper carburetor adjustment. The first problem is the most common and the easiest to check. Remove the air cleaner and take a gauge reading. If the needle doesn't rise and then remain steady, make sure the carburetor float isn't sticking or out of adjustment. If it checks out, adjust the carburetor idle-mixture screw for the highest steady gauge reading and then back off until

the reading drops a half in. Set the idle-speed screw so the engine doesn't stall on sudden braking or, in the case of a stick-shift car, when the clutch is disengaged. If your car has an automatic transmission, set the idle speed low enough to prevent creeping in Drive.

**If the pointer drifts** over one or two in., say between 15 and 16, don't blame the carburetor. Spark-plug gaps may be set too close or ignition points may be matched improperly. To check for defective spark plugs, short each one in turn with an insulated screwdriver. If the plug is good the reading should drop about one-half to one in. A defective plug will not affect the reading at all. A plug may fire at low speed but cut out at higher speeds so run this test both at idle and at high rpm.

A drop of two or more in. at regular intervals while the engine is idling means a valve isn't seating properly—a dangerous condition. The vacuum reading isn't affected until the intake valve in that cylinder opens. At that time, exhaust gases leak in and reduce vacuum. The defective valve will need refacing and reseating.

A sticking valve will cause an occasional but rapid drop of about four in. To find the bad valve, squirt a few drops of penetrating oil into each valve guide. When you come to the sticking valve the gauge reading will steady itself temporarily.

A regular drop of about six in. means a burned valve. It must be replaced.

A fast vibration between 14 and 19 in. indicates loose or worn valve guides that must be replaced. Weak valve springs don't show up at idle but the gauge registers a wide vibration when the throttle is opened quickly.

**Shut off the engine** and remove the distributor cap so the engine won't fire. When you crank the engine with the starter, you should get a reading of about five in. A lower reading indicates a leak between the intake and exhaust manifolds.

Replace the distributor cap and start the engine. If the gauge shows a normal reading at first, then drops to zero and climbs slowly to a reading slightly lower than normal, the exhaust system probably is blocked partially. This could mean shifted packing in the muffler. •

# THE REAL STORY ON GAUGES

## Are idiot lights for the bright and dials for the dumb?
## Do tachs & temp gauges talk sense? You find out here!

WHY install gauges when I have warning lights?

Sound familiar? Both the answer and a measure of the relative importance of gauges may be had by peering into the cockpit of a competition car. Here you'll find a tachometer placed right in front of the driver, often up near his line of vision. Clustered around the tach are other gauges: oil-temperature, oil-pressure, water-temperature.

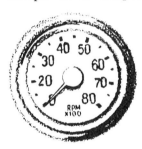

**A TACH for a slush-box? Its uses are many.**

Don't be surprised at the absence of a speedometer. The experienced competition driver is interested only in the power output and operating condition of his engine.

Aren't we all interested in the performance of our autos? Even more important, instead of depending upon a 9¢ lamp to show something is definitely wrong, don't we want to detect trouble ahead of time and prevent major breakdowns?

*That* is the reason for installing gauges, even in a slush-box six. For proper interpretation of instruments results in peak performance of any engine.

**Next question:** Fine, I should have some gauges. But which ones and how much will they cost and can I install them myself and what should I look for

and how can I interpret the readings?

Truthfully, the answer varies somewhat with each combination of driver and auto. However, since a driver should know the condition of his electrical and oil systems at all times, an ammeter or voltmeter is a basic must, as is an oil-temperature or pressure gauge. From these, drivers can extend instrumentation by adding some other gauges we shall discuss. In either case, the average motorist can become a confident driver by using his gauges (and his head) to feel the pulse of his auto.

**Tachometers**—There are two basic types of tachometer: electrically operated and mechanically driven. The mechanical type usually is connected by a rotating cable from the dash to a gear housing near the distributor shaft. The electrically operated tach is powered by pulses from the distributor and is easier to install since only a single wire is required. (Un-

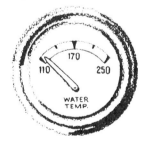

**USE this and watch the other guy steam.**

less factory-fitted with a suitable connector, most cars will not accept a mechanically-driven tach.)

When shopping for a tach look both for an angular indicating span of at least 180° and an illuminated scale. Make certain the rpm range is neither too high nor too low for your car's engine. Don't get a unit with a cluttered face—four divisions per thousand rpm is sufficient. This way, at high speeds, a glance will be enough to get a clear reading. If your car is fitted with transistor ignition, make certain the tach will work with a transistor system.

When equipping a stick-shift job with a tach, set your own upper limits and abide by them. Draw a red line on the face-plate of the tach to correspond with tested shift points. On automatics,

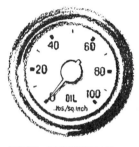

the red markings also can be used as an indication of transmission operation—it may be shifting too soon or too late. The tach also will show if and when the automatic bands start slipping.

**HIGH PRESSURE is trouble; can't light light.**

Use the tach when setting idle speed. You also can use the tach to check the accuracy of your speedometer. For example, assume your 6-cylinder car with a 3.11 final ratio does 21.2 mph per 1,000 rpm. Thus, holding steady at 3,000 rpm in fourth should produce a speedometer reading of 63.6 mph. Your service manual or dealer can be checked for the speed of your auto at 1,000 rpm (specify in top gear).

You should expect to pay anywhere from $20 to $45 for a tach, depending on range and make.

**Water Temperature**—Electrical temperature gauges consist basically of a transmitting element and an indicating gauge, connected by a single wire. Some engines have a plug provided on the thermostat housing in addition to the one for the warning light's sensing element. If not, a T adapter can be used to install transmitters for both lamp and gauge.

The gauge can be used to reveal a defective thermostat (high reading when running, extremely low reading for a long warm-up period). A high indication also may result from an overworked engine, low water level, loose or slipping water-pump belt, leaky hose or radiator or a faulty water pump.

The recommended range for a water-temperature gauge is about 250°F. Again, make a red or green sector extending from lowest to highest normal operating temperatures. When you see the indicator above or below the colored sector pull over immediately and inspect the cooling system. For the initial outlay of $9 to $12, this gauge can turn out to be worth its weight in gold.

**Oil Pressure**—The simplest type of oil pressure gauge consists of a transmitter and dashboard gauge connected by a single wire. Installation is simple for the transmitter is adapted to the plug originally used for the warning light. (Wherever possible, it is advisable to use both the indicating gauge and warning light.) This plug usually is located on the side of the main block and is found by tracing the wires from the dash.

A low pressure reading may be due to a low oil level in the crankcase, faulty oil filter, frothing of the oil, an unusually hot engine or a defective pressure-regulator valve. Depending on location, a clogged oil line can produce either low or high readings. If this possibility exists, flush the oil system as soon as possible, clean or change the filter and make certain the new oil is of the correct weight for the particular season and operating conditions.

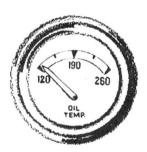

**TAKES TIME to install but can save overhaul.**

Cost? A good oil-pressure gauge with a full scale of about 0 to 80 lbs. per sq. in. will cost $10 to $15.

**Oil Temperature**—Installing the transmitter for an oil temperature gauge usually requires drilling and mounting the transmitter in the lower side of the oil pan and running a lead from pan to the dash. This bit of elbow grease is well worthwhile when you consider that a hot engine means thin oil and thin oil heats the engine further, which thins the oil even more, etc., until the lubricant, followed by the engine, breaks down.

Another important reason for an oil-temperature gauge is that the warning light normally provided does not present a true indication of the oil system's condition. In some cases, oil pressure may be sufficient to keep the light from turning on, even though the oil has lost most of its lubricating property. The importance of an oil-temperature gauge cannot be overstressed—remember, only relatively cool oil is an effective lubricant. For the $10 to $15 an oil-temp gauge costs, you may avoid paying for a major overhaul.

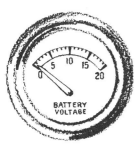

**READ 14 or 15 volts and know charging is good.**

When choosing a gauge look for one with a full scale of at least 250°F. After installation, watch it carefully for a week or two, then mark the upper and lower temperatures you've observed. If the needle later falls outside this sector, check your oil and water levels. (If your initial readings seem abnormal, call your dealer and ask for the factory-recommended limits. You may have problems already!)

**Ammeters/Voltmeters**—Either type of meter will provide a good indication of the electrical system's condition. Installation is fairly simple. An ammeter is connected in series between the battery and generator or alternator, while a voltmeter is connected in parallel with the battery. (Although these are the electrical connection points, their physical location often is at more convenient junctions.) Always make sure the wire used to connect an ammeter is of sufficient size to carry the current safely.

Select an ammeter with a 40-amp range for the average car and 60 amps for cars equipped with air conditioners. Prices range anywhere from $2.50 to $4.50.

Turning the starter should produce a surge of current in the discharge direction, followed by a surge in the opposite, or charge, direction when the car is started. The needle then will drop gradually to a slight charge indication if the system is operating properly. If irregularities are detected, first check the generator drive belt, the voltage regulator, the water level in the battery and, if necessary, the fuses and their connections.

A voltmeter also costs about $5 and, like an ammeter, it shows how well your electrical system is operating. For a 12-volt system, the reading should be 12 volts with the engine off and the ignition turned on. After ten minutes of driving battery voltage should increase to 14 or 15 volts if the charging system is working properly. Draw a red sector between 12 to 15 volts and you have an excellent warning device—when you see the arrow stop and check out the system.

**In addition** to the types of meters and gauges we've discussed, there are innumerable variations on the accessory market. These vary in both purpose and validity, ranging from gas and mileage computators on to esoteric accelerometers. Needles to say, prices are correspondingly astronomical and, for all practical purposes, these devices are not for us.

Although we've spoken in terms of individual gauges, bear in mind that combination gauges generally are just

**It should go down, up, then down again. Phew!**

as accurate, require less space and often will cost less than two single gauges.

But the instruments we've described, coupled with a bit of analytical thinking will help transform an average motorist into a diagnostic driver. (Author's definition: The diagnostic driver is one who does not feel that the $500 engine in his $3,000 car should be entrusted to, or dependent upon, the functioning of 9¢ lamps.) •

LOOSEN all the head bolts or nuts in a 10-1 sequence. Follow order of 1-10 to tighten.

# A VALVE JOB FOR $20

*With a minimum of time and expense, owners of overhead-valve engines can do their own valve jobs. The key: organized labor.*

THE mere mention of a valve job seems to be enough to send most motorists into a state of anxiety and apprehension. Aside from the exorbitant expenses involved, there also is an understandable aversion to giving up the buggy for three or four days.

Yet the average Saturday wrench-twirler, by using a straightforward approach, can do a first-rate job in half the time and for a fraction of the normal fee. How? Simply by removing the cylinder heads himself, trotting them down to the nearest automotive machine shop and having the shop complete the job of grinding and reseating the valves, often on a while-you-wait basis. Reverse these steps and your job is completed.

**Total cost?** Expect to pay a machinist $12 to $18 for reworking a V-6 and about $18 to $24 for a V-8. Add the price of a gasket set ($3 to $9) and your total outlay ranges from $15 to $33, quite a drop from a fee of $70 to $100.

The time involved also is decreased from the mechanic's three or four days to six to 15 hours, usually broken into two sessions. However, by making an appointment with a good machinist, the entire job can be completed in one day.

**Why a valve job?** Valves control the cycling of each cylinder. Thus, if an exhaust valve is leaking due to carbon build-up or faulty seating power from each combustion cycle will be lost through the exhaust port. Similarly, if the inlet valve is leaking fuel consumption increases greatly without an increase in power output. In this case, flooding, difficulty in starting and knocking usually result. Either way, valves are important and require more atten-

1. DRAIN radiator, disconnect all hoses at intake manifold and swing out of way.

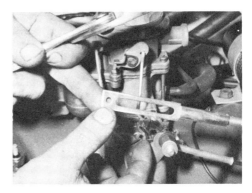

2. REMOVE the throttle linkage, making as few disconnections as possible. Keep notes.

tion than usually is accorded them.

As a rule of thumb, about once a year or every 30,000 miles, pull a valve job. Begin with the following:

• Collect a set of standard wrenches, a screwdriver, torque wrench, scraper and wire brush.

• Dig around for a package of envelopes or small plastic bags, a bunch of tags or labels with tape or wire ties and a pad and pencil.

• Call an automotive machine shop and set an appointment for Saturday afternoon.

• Get a good night's sleep Friday.

**Ready?** Disconnect the battery cables, drain the cooling system and remove the air cleaner. Disconnect the upper radiator hose and any heater hose that goes into the cylinder head, intake manifold or thermostat housing. Leave the clamps on the hoses so you'll have them at reassembly time.

Now remove the rocker cover(s). Place the nuts or bolts and washers in a bag and label the bag, leaving it in one of the rocker covers.

The next step is to disconnect the throttle linkage from the carburetor. While linkage setups vary, these general guidelines hold for all types of autos:

• Make a sketch of the linkage layout. Even if the arrangement looks simple, by the time you're ready for reassembly you may have forgotten it.

• Disconnect as little as possible. Two or three disconnections will do it

3. DISCONNECT fuel line at carburetor or filter. Swing it out of the way; don't bend.

every time. After a disconnection try to refit pins and clips in the slots or holes from which they came to ease reassembly. If this isn't possible put the bits and pieces and your sketch into a labeled bag.

Disconnect the fuel line at the carburetor or fuel filter, then loosen it at the fuel pump and try to swing it out of the way. If you can't remove the line. Take care not to bond the copper tubing.

Inspect the intake manifold to see whether there's anything else bolted to it (such as a ground strap) or something strung over it (wires, hoses, etc.). To avoid confusion, tag each hose and its connection point as you disconnect.

The intake manifold should be removed with the carburetor left in place. If the ignition coil is mounted on the in-

**4. REMOVE bolts holding intake manifold. Compare the size and length of the bolts.**

**5. COMPLETE any further disconnections and remove the intake manifold carefully.**

take manifold just disconnect the wires. Tag each of the two thin wires as you remove them, labeling them with the sign on the coil terminal (usually a plus or minus sign or a letter). Refit the terminal mounting nuts so they don't get lost.

Remove the intake-manifold bolts and swing away anything held to those bolts, such as a throttle-linkage bracket. Then pull off the intake manifold.

The next step usually is generator removal. Even if it is not bolted to the cylinder head it will interfere with head removal on V-8s. You may not have to

pull the generator on a Six so check before you unbolt.

At this point, you have to decide whether to pull the exhaust manifold with the head. This is the usual procedure but it requires disconnecting the exhaust manifold from the exhaust pipe, probably from underneath the car. If this appears difficult unbolt the manifold from the head, pull it away from the head and rethread the nuts or bolts into the head.

Before removing the manifold from the head you probably will have to pull off the spark-plug wires. Otherwise, you can wait until later. Make a layout drawing of the spark plugs, numbering them any way you want so long as you put a number tag on each wire to conform with your drawing.

**At this point** you're ready to pull the heads. First loosen the bolts or stud nuts, starting with No. 10 as shown in our illustration and proceeding to No. 1. Place them in a labeled bag. On engines with bolts, remove the bolts one at a time and check length. If any are longer than others, make a sketch of bolt locations so you can reinstall them properly.

Remove the rocker assembly. On engines with all rockers in-line on a shaft, don't disturb the rocker adjusting nuts or screws and when you reassemble, valve adjustments will be close.

On engines with non-adjustable rockers, individually mounted or in-line on a shaft, remove and label the shaft or rocker—no settings to disturb.

Now check the highly-popular exception: hydraulic lifters and individually mounted adjustable rockers, used on most Chevy V-8s and some Fords. In this case mark one flat of the rocker's adjusting nut with nail polish and then unscrew it, counting the exact number of turns for each nut. Keep each rocker and nut together in a separate envelope labeled as to exact location on which head. You'll be able to refit them close enough to get the engine running. Final adjustments are explained later.

**After the rocker** assembly and pushrods have been removed the head should be loose on the block. If not, try to break it loose by prying *the outside* or *body of the head* with a large screwdriver. *Do not insert the screwdriver between head and block.* If there's any real resistance odds are there's a nut or bolt still in place.

After the machine shop is done with the valve part of the job, clean carbon and lead deposits from the combustion chamber, using a wire brush—either hand or electric-drill type. To clean the piston tops, use a scraper with care.

**Now you're ready** for reassembly, a reversal of disassembly with some important additions.

Scrape all gasket surfaces until clean. Coat both sides of the cylinder-head gasket with a sparing amount of nonhardening sealer and place it on the block. Move the cylinder head into place, then fit the push rods into the lifters at one end and into the rocker seat at the other. Thread in the head bolts and run them down finger tight.

You'll need tightening specifications for the head and rockers. Check your service manual (or ask the machine shop or your auto dealer's service department).

Start by tightening the bolts for the rocker shaft (or the nuts for individually mounted rockers), using a torque wrench on all but adjustable hydraulic arrangements. In this case, turn down each nut the number of turns taken to remove it.

Reversing the removal sequence (start with No. 1, proceed to No. 10) tighten the head bolts slowly, a couple of turns on each bolt at a time in the beginning. This will prevent squashing the lifters or bending the pushrods. Once the head is fully seated use the torque wrench to tighten the head to factory specifications. Tighten the head bolts or nuts in progressive stages. For example, if the setting is 70 ft.-lbs., tighten all bolts first to 25, then 50 and finally 70.

It's primarily straight nuts-and-bolts work from here, reconnecting everything that was disconnected. If you have been careful and made sketches you'll have all parts and know where they go.

**Now for the final** valve settings on those cars with adjustable lifters. Engines with solid lifters demand a special

6. REMOVE head bolts and rocker assembly. Take out pushrods, unseat head carefully.

7. REMOVE head and deliver to machinist. Use care not to strike machined surface.

technique. If you don't know how, leave the job to a professional, who should get $2.50 to $4 for the job.

If your engine has adjustable hydraulic lifters, run the engine at a slow idle. Turn the adjusting nut counterclockwise until the valves starts to clatter, then clockwise until the clatter just disappears. Turn an additional 1½ turns on Fords and one additional turn on Chevrolets.

Refit the valve covers and you'll have a valve job done as well as any professional shop could do it—certainly for a lot less money. •

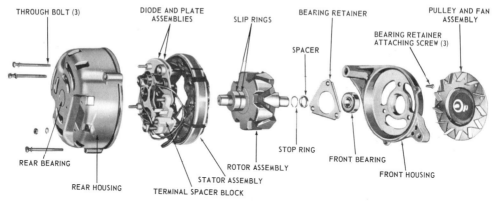

THROUGH BOLT (3)     DIODE AND PLATE ASSEMBLIES     SLIP RINGS     BEARING RETAINER     PULLEY AND FAN ASSEMBLY

BEARING RETAINER ATTACHING SCREW (3)

SPACER

REAR BEARING     STOP RING     FRONT BEARING

ROTOR ASSEMBLY     FRONT HOUSING

REAR HOUSING     STATOR ASSEMBLY

TERMINAL SPACER BLOCK

Courtesy Autolite Division, Ford Motor Co.

# The TROUBLE
# With ALTERNATORS

THE ALTERNATOR, together with the battery and voltage regulator, make up the charging circuit of most recent-model cars. When hooked up properly, these three units act as a team to supply energy for the entire system. But the alternator, successor to the conventional DC generator, is a sensitive apparatus and there are a number of things that can go wrong with it.

What can you do to get top results from the alternator? Simplest maintenance of all is to check for a worn, loose or glazed alternator drive belt.

The specialty of the alternator or AC generator is its ability to keep the battery fully charged even at low engine speeds, a desirable feature that helps handle the heavy electrical loads encountered in stop-and-go driving, especially in winter. But belt slippage continues to be a big factor in low output and battery weakness—with all of the resulting woes.

**Another common problem** is a shorted diode. While an alternator produces alternating current this is con-verted to DC by means of silicon diodes (rectifiers) which allow current to pass in one direction but not in the other. If one of the diodes is shorted, allowing current to flow in either direction, this will show up as reduced output some ten amperes below rated capacity. This may explain why the battery doesn't stay charged.

One clue to a shorted diode is a tendency for the alternator to whine, especially at engine idle. Thousands of alternators have been replaced just because mechanics have mistaken this noise for evidence of more serious trouble.

An open-circuit diode will not allow current to flow in either direction. The usual clue here is an output of two to five amps less than specification.

While diodes can prove troublesome, they are replaceable and manufacturers compete in an effort to make these little electrical devices as sturdy as possible. Delco-Remy tests them at production time by connecting random-selected diodes to special equipment and immersing them in a 70° water bath. The diode

IF indicator lamp on dash remains on when it should go off connect voltmeter from alternator's R terminal to ground with engine running. Reading over five volts means the lamp relay is fauty; reading under five volts points to alternator trouble.

is then jolted with 62.5 amps (2½ times normal intensity) for five seconds. Current is turned off and the diode's internal temperature drops from around 350°F to 100°F. The cycle is repeated 1,750 times, representing more stress than the diode would receive in a car's lifetime.

**If the alternator** is thought to be op-

erating normally but the battery doesn't receive enough juice it's reasonable to suspect the regulator or wiring. But first make sure the culprit isn't the luggage compartment light staying on with the lid closed or that an excessive amount of current isn't otherwise being consumed by the car's electrical equipment.

The only function of the regulator used with the alternator is to limit DC output voltage. It performs its function by sensing the voltage output of the AC generator and then regulating the generator field current. Poor grounding, due to loose or corroded terminals, is a common cause of regulator trouble. And if a fuse wire is used in the circuit, merely replacing this often will keep the regulator going.

In all alternator testing it is important to have the battery fully charged. When using a fast charger the battery's cables must be disconnected. Only exception is where the charger has an alternator protector. In using booster wires from another car's battery the cables must be connected in parallel. That is, the plus of the helper battery is connected to the plus of the ailing one and minus to minus.

At this point it should be noted that

ROTOR WINDING of Delcotron AC generator may be checked for grounds by connecting the leads from a simple 1½-volt test lamp or an ohmmeter to either slip ring and the shaft. Test lamp will light if the rotor winding is shorted. A high ohmmeter reading indicates the winding is good, whereas a low reading indicates a short.

DIODES can be tested, using a test lamp with battery voltage of not more than 12 volts. Connect one of the test leads to the diode lead and the other to the diode case. Then reverse the connections. If the lamp lights or fails to light in both checks the diode is defective. The lamp should light in only one of the two diode checks.

a short circuit through the diodes is created if the battery is installed and connected with ground polarity reversed. Alternators run clockwise and are negative-grounded. Reversed polarity not only will damage the alternator's rectifiers but the regulator as well.

**Cooling the alternator** is important. That's why there are impeller blades on either side of the rotor and a ventilated shield encases the entire unit.

Because it is exposed to road splash there's much to be said for cleaning the exterior of the alternator and taking steps to prevent dirt from getting inside. Sometimes it's a good idea to shield the alternator. If the car is to be driven through deep puddles, go slowly to avoid excessive splash.

If you just want to find out how well the alternator is doing you can use a voltmeter to test. Using a Delcotron AC generator by way of illustration, first disconnect the four-terminal connector at the regulator and the two-terminal connector at the alternator. Next step is to connect a jumper between the battery and field terminals of the alternator. Now connect the voltmeter to the battery terminal and the ground terminal. Start the engine and turn on the heater's blower and high-beam headlights as an accessory load. Output should exceed 12.5 volts within a few minutes with the engine operating at 1,500 rpm. Anything below 12.5 volts signals trouble and calls for a closer look.

**One of the first steps** in dismantling an alternator is to remove the brushes so as to avoid damaging them. Each brush is mounted in a plastic holder which positions it against one of two slip rings. Naturally a wobbly ring can prove troublesome. Ford limits the amount of allowable run-out to .0005 in. If a slip ring is damaged or can't be trued by taking a light cut from its face, Ford recommends rotor replacement.

If the stator assembly needs cleaning use a cloth dampened with turpentine. The same applies to cleaning the rotor. Rotate the rotor while cleaning the slip rings. Brush noise may be the penalty for flat spots on the rings. Never use sandpaper on rings. Clean and polish with coarse denim.

**It is important** to have specific instructions before anything beyond general alternator care is attempted. Even minor variations between Chrysler, Ford, Delco-Remy (Delcotron), Motorola, Prestolite and Leece-Neville systems can cause problems.

On the Motorola system, for example, there's an isolation diode which doesn't play any role in rectifying AC current. One of its functions is to connect the voltage regulator to the alternator and battery automatically. Another role is to check electrical leakage over the alternator's insulation.

To test for an open field or short circuit in a Ford alternator, connect a test ammeter to the positive post of the battery and to the alternator's frame. With another connection between the battery's negative post and the alternator's field terminal normal current draw for the 1965 Ford engine should be 2.8 to 3.3 amps at 12 volts and 75°F. But if there is no flow, or too little, chances are there's a high resistance or an open circuit. Or the brushes may not be contacting the slip rings properly. If current flow is too high you'll know there's shorted or grounded wiring in the field.

**While most** alternator problems involve undercharging there are plenty of instances of overcharging. Stuck contacts in the regulator can cause the latter condition. And don't be too ready to condemn the alternator if suddenly there's no charging. The fuse may be blown or the fusible wire burned out.

Watch for the simple things when the alternator seems to be laying down on the job. Excessive resistance in the circuits between the alternator and the battery or between the battery and the ground often is mistaken for more serious problems. And many a noisy alternator has been replaced simply because is was loose or its rotor fan was hitting some part of the assembly. •

# Installing Your Own Seat Covers

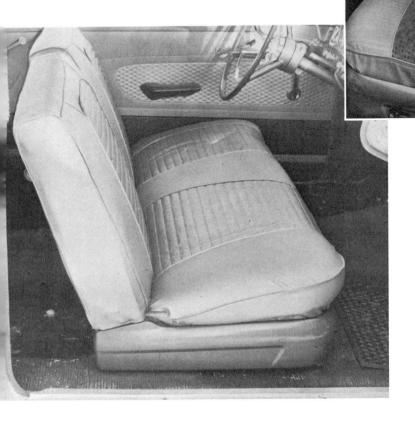

SEAT COVERS are the most abused part of your car's interior. New covers are inexpensive, easy to install and boost resale value. Before and after shots show the extent of transformation.

IF the seat covers in your car look like they have been through a meat grinder, try re-covering them. It's easier than you may think. Not only will new covers add to the beauty of your car, but you'll increase the resale value too.

Seat covers are available in various price ranges. You can get low cost stretch covers in terry cloth or nylon knit. These are washable and they range from a low of about $5 per seat to around $12. The embossed vinyls are next. These start at $12 per seat. The top quality covers run between $15 to $20 per seat. These are made of fabric-reinforced vinyl and they are crease- as

well as wear-resistant; your best bet.

When you purchase seat covers installed, the installation charges are included in the price. This charge may run as high as $20. You can save a nice piece of change by doing the work yourself. All you need in the way of tools is a screwdriver, pliers and a special hog ring pliers plus a box of hog rings. The hog rings look like oversize staples and they are used for fastening the upholstery to the seat frame. You can get the special pliers and a box of rings for $2 at most auto supply shops.

Start by removing the seat side wings and all hardware which will interfere

1. REMOVE seat adjustment lever, if necessary, so you can remove the side wings.

2. SIDE WINGS must be removed carefully to avoid bending them out of shape.

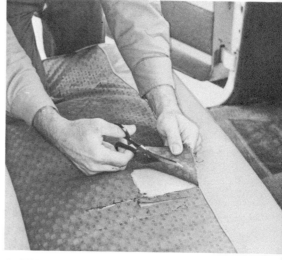

3. BACK REST on folding seats should be removed. Don't lose any of the hardware.

4. TRIM torn fabric and loose piping so it won't become a bulge under new covers.

with the covers. If the front seats are the tilting type, they can be removed to facilitate the re-covering. The rear seats in all cars are removable. The rear back rest is usually held by two bolts, screwed into the trunk wall, or by means of a pair of clips.

If the old upholstery has tears or loose ends and patches, cut them off or they'll make lumps under the new covers. In most cases piping can be left intact, but if it is ripped or frayed it would be advisable to remove the damaged part. If the piping is exceptionally high, it should be removed entirely. Use a razor blade to cut through the stitching.

On older cars the front seat may sag excessively due to spring fatigue, but you can pad it with foam to bring it back to its original shape and size. Either polyurethane or foam rubber may be used. The foam—which should be at least 1 in. thick—is placed on the seat and trimmed to size. Make the cut about 1 in. oversize all around.

The actual covering is rather simple. The important thing to remember is that the material must be pulled *tightly and evenly*. Always work from the center out. Fasten the material with the hog rings. Use as many rings as you like. If you make an error, snip the ring and

5. FOAM PAD, at least 1-in. thick, aids sagging seats. Cut it slightly oversize.

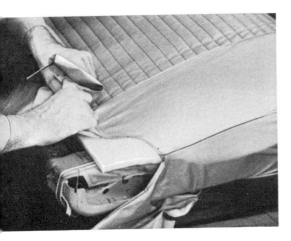

6. STRETCH cover tightly over seat and pad. Seam should reach back edge of seat.

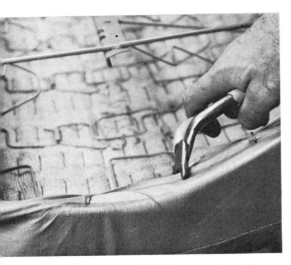

7. HOG RINGS hold fabric in place. Use as many as you need to remove all wrinkles.

# Seat Covers

insert another. A good trick is to squeeze the seat when installing the rings for a nice tight fit.

If the weather is cold be sure to keep the covers in a warm room until ready to use, especially vinyls and vinyl-clad materials.

**If your seats are an odd** shape or size, you may be able to alter a standard set of covers to fit. You will need a sewing machine, a steam iron, some tailors' chalk and a set of covers slightly larger than your seats. The steam iron is used only on plastic covers and only as a source of steam. The iron should not be applied directly to the material as most plasticized fabric will be ruined by such action. The steam makes the material pliable so it can be worked more easily.

Most fitting will be found necessary on the seat backs. Seat bottoms are fairly standard and you should have no difficulty on this score.

Place the cover on the seat and note where the loose areas start and stop. Make small reference marks with the chalk, then remove the cover. Now carefully open up the seam using a scissor or razor blade. If the cover has piping, be careful not to damage it as you will need to reuse it.

**Replace the cover and pin** along the new seam line. Steam the fabric to render it pliable and pull it tightly together as you pin. When fully pinned, the cover should fit snugly. If some parts are too loose or too tight, repin until the cover appears perfect. The final results will be only as good as the pinning.

Note the original seam allowance and allow the same on the new section. Trim the excess then turn the covers inside out and repin on the wrong side. Using a long stitch, sew along the pin line. You can sew right over the pins removing them after you are done. If the cover had piping, be sure to replace it before sewing.

On non-plastic covers, the procedure is the same except that the steaming is eliminated. •

# Driving Habits
# can ruin your car!

STRANGE how unlucky some motorists are. Every car they buy is a lemon. But tell them that their driving may be at fault and they'll insist they're the most careful drivers around. They *always* warm up a cold engine. They *never* drive a car hard.

Wrong!, say top automotive engineers. In recent years they've blasted these and other old-wives' tales that careful drivers hold dear. Fact is, an automotive hypochondriac usually does more harm than good.

Take, for example, the eager-beaver driver who's so anxious to break in his new car that he takes it on a several-hundred-mile trip. The owner's manual recommends a maximum of 50 mph during break-in so he keeps the speedometer glued to 50. Or maybe he's conservative and holds a steady 40. In either event, he's making a mistake. His engine parts never will seat correctly. Instead, he should be varying his speed and increasing the maximum speed gradually by about 5 mph every 100 miles.

**Few people** realize they should lift the foot off the gas completely every few minutes during break-in. This sucks oil up the cylinder walls for much-needed lubrication that helps piston rings to seat properly.

Also, a car must be broken in all over again if *any* of its running gear (engine, transmission, clutch, rear end, etc.) is rebuilt or replaced.

It's true that until a few years ago owner manuals recommended idling a cold engine until it reached normal operating temperature. But for one thing, a five-minute warmup twice a day, every day, adds up to over 60 hours a year. That's two and a half full days of running!

But besides wasting time, this actually can harm the engine. A cool engine needs all the lubrication it can get—and oil pressure is lowest at idle. Also, an engine running in Neutral literally shakes itself to death. Driving off cold, on the other hand, puts a load on the engine and makes it run smoother.

In fact, you'd have a good argument if you said an engine with an automatic transmission lasts longer than one with a stick shift because, instead of being in Neutral at every stop, it is almost always in gear and under load.

The only time there's any excuse for warming up a car is if you live near a turnpike and don't want to subject a cold engine to high revs. And then you should leave the engine in Drive and hold down on the brake pedal when you warm it up to keep it under load.

On cold mornings, one engineer we know, when he wants engine heat for the heater, sets the parking brake, chocks one of the wheels and leaves his car idling in Drive while he finishes his coffee. But he hesitates to recommend this practice to anyone else. "If you do try it," he says, "make damn sure your parking brake is good."

Everyone knows that a cold engine shouldn't be run too fast but few know when an engine is warm. Forget about the water-temperature gauge. The important factor is oil temperature. You can drive safely at moderate turnpike speeds after two or three miles, gradually increasing speed until you've covered about ten miles—the distance it takes for the oil to warm up fully.

Hard driving doesn't hurt. The idea that the most desirable used car was owned by a little old school teacher is as out-of-date as ankle-length skirts. Fast turnpike driving is far better for your engine than slow, short-haul city driving. At high speeds water that has condensed in the engine oil boils away and carbon deposits don't build up as quickly. (But not too fast, please.)

In fact, if most of your driving is stop-and-go, your engine will benefit from a good, hard high-speed run every few weeks. If speed limits are low in your area you can get pretty much the same results by running at lower speed in low gear.

The only kind of hard driving that does harm your car is making abrupt changes in speed or direction. Wheel-spinning acceleration and panic stops are rough on running gear and hard cornering plays havoc with tires, suspension and steering. A good driver thinks ahead and plans his course so he can maintain a steady speed, not only because it's easier on the machinery but also because he'll make better time that way.

**Knowing how** to change gears can save you some mighty big repair bills. An automatic transmission does most of the thinking for you so there are just a few things to worry about. The most important is to make certain the car isn't rolling forward when you shift into Reverse or rolling backward when you shift into a forward gear. When you rock your car out of a snow drift, don't shift back and forth from Drive to Reverse. Decide which direction offers the best chance of pulling out. If it's forward, shift into a forward gear—if it's backward, shift into reverse. Accelerate gently, then let the car roll back and accelerate again to clear a path.

Avoid shifting an automatic manually unless you're creeping in slow traffic and want to prevent an upshift. Even for all-out acceleration there is little advantage in shifting manually and, unless you have a reliable tachometer, you risk overrevving the engine.

**A manual transmission** demands considerably more skill. A stock-car racing driver claims that only one stick-shift driver out of a hundred can shift properly.

First you must know *when* to shift. Too low a gear wastes gas and risks overrevving. Too high a gear—a far

ROLLING INTO A CURB this way is bound to damage the tire carcass. In addition, this will knock front wheels out of line.

DRIVE FRONT WHEELS on newspaper when servicing car. This will make turning steering wheel easier, less strain on system.

STEEP HILL with stop at end? Shift into lower gear and apply steady brake pressure rather than pumping, unless road is icy.

PARK WIPERS when you turn engine off, else next time you start the engine, wipers will scratch the glass and strain the motor.

UNAVOIDABLE POTHOLE? Brake to slow as much as possible, then lift your foot just before you hit hole to prevent wheel lock-up.

more common mistake—risks chugging and damage from detonation. Shifting too often adds unnecessary wear to the clutch, transmission and other parts of the driveline and is one of several bad habits that can ruin a car.

How often you should shift depends mainly on the power-to-weight ratio and the gearing of your car. With a small, low-power engine you have to shift more frequently. But it's a good rule of thumb that no car should be driven around a right corner on city streets in high gear. Left corners can be run faster because of the greater ra-

dius, so with a big engine you may be able to get away with high gear.

A common error is keeping the car in gear while waiting for a light. Holding the clutch disengaged can cause severe wear of the clutch throw-out bearing. Instead stay in Neutral and watch the light controlling cross-traffic. When it turns amber it's time for you to shift into first.

Members of the sporty-car set often are guilty of using the transmission to stop the car. They'll shift down through all the gears just to come to a stop directly ahead. A wise friend of ours says:

"I'd much rather pay for new brake linings than a new transmission or clutch."

Downshift not to slow but to be in the proper gear when it's time to accelerate.

Skipping gears or shifting from first to third widens the gap between ratios and greatly increases the load on the transmission synchronizers. The only exception is in downshifting—so long as you're on expert at double-clutching.

**No, double-clutching** didn't go out with the nonsynchronized (crashbox) transmission of years ago. Double-clutching is an absolute must when shifting into a nonsynchronized low gear while you're moving. Proper double-clutching during *all* downshifts can double or triple the life of a transmission.

It takes practice. First you disengage the clutch, shift into neutral and re-engage the clutch. Then you blip the throttle, again disengage the clutch and shift into a lower gear. The blip speeds up the transmission gears for smooth meshing. It's not necessary during upshifts because the gear speed drops when the clutch is disengaged.

**To prolong clutch life** avoid using the pedal as a foot rest. When shifting, push the pedal *all* the way down. Avoid slipping the clutch or holding it partially engaged.

For years drivers have been pumping brakes when descending steep slopes. This was supposed to admit cool air into the drums and prevent overheating and fade.

Well, it's just not true. Recent tests indicate that pumping builds up more energy, thereby increasing heat, fade and lining wear. The car will accelerate slightly between brake applications, so the brakes have to work that much harder. Pumping is useful only on slippery road surfaces, where it gives better steering control.

On long descents it's wise to downshift instead and use engine braking to avoid running out of brakes. This is especially true with automatic-transmission cars, which practically freewheel in Drive. Here you have to shift the automatic manually.

The large brake pedals on automatic-transmission cars tempt many motorists to brake with the left foot. Supporters of this practice claim it's faster than lifting the right foot off the throttle. The Ford Motor Co., however, recently made motion pictures timed to a thousandth of a second to prove there is no significant difference in reaction times.

Also, many engineers believe that left-foot brakers unconsciously use their brakes more and tend to use the pedal as a foot rest. And few people have as much dexterity in the left foot as in the right.

Another modern convenience indirectly responsible for repair bills is power steering. It's all too easy for drivers to turn the steering wheel with the car motionless, a practice that places a tremendous strain on the steering system. It's smart to let the car roll slowly while turning the wheel. If you service your own car and it becomes necessary to turn the front wheels back and forth, drive the wheels onto several sheets of newspaper to reduce friction between tires and ground.

**Bumping the curb** when parking diagonally not only damages tires but also can knock the front end badly out of line. Large potholes can do the same. If you see one in time, drive around it. If you can't avoid it, slow down as much as possible but get off the brakes just before you hit. If you keep the brakes applied the wheel will lock up as it drops into the hole and hit the far edge much harder than if it were free to roll. The same advice holds for train tracks and bumps in the road.

**It's best** to stay off bad roads entirely. Not only are they hard on the suspension and body panels but country roads cut tire life by as much as one half. On crushed-stone roads, your tires can wear out five times faster than they would on asphalt.

On hot days and in heavy traffic, watch your water-temperature gauge or warning light. If the temperature rises too high, turn on the heater. It may be uncomfortable but it will draw away some of engine heat. If you're stopped in bumper-to-bumper traffic, *don't* shut off the engine for short periods—the coolant stops circulating and the temperature rises. Instead, rev up your engine—the radiator fan will turn faster and bring the temperature down. •

# What to do When a Car Won't Start

AN engine that won't start needn't mushroom into lost time, great expense or a migraine headache. In just a few minutes, you usually can isolate the faulty component. Then nine out of ten times you'll find you can correct the problem without even rolling up your shirt sleeves.

The successful procedure lies in analyzing the first symptom—does it or doesn't it crank?

**If the engine won't crank**—When you turn the key to the *on* position the red ignition light on your dash also should go on, indicating the ignition switch is good and the battery is putting out enough to power the lamp. If the lamp remains off try a short blast on the horn or turn on the lights. There's always the chance that the bulb has burned out.

In the event all these circuits prove inoperative, check the battery and its connections—there should be electrolyte in each of the battery's cells and the cable connectors should be tight. Check the ground connection.

If you're lucky enough to have a hydrometer at hand, use it to check the battery charge. If this is all right, then rumple your suit by peering under the dash and removing the fuse-box cover. While there, you also might look for loose cables. Pull each fuse in turn and hold it to the sunlight or a flashlight to ascertain continuity. If you can identify the ignition-circuit fuse, of course, you need check only that one.

Take one giant step and turn the ignition key to *start* position. You first should hear the starter solenoid fall in with a solid click. If you have an automatic transmission and the engine fails to crank, try starting in both the N and P positions. Jiggle the gear selector a bit—there's a neutral safety switch (for starting only in these two positions) that may have worked loose or failed.

Then if the starter still fails to crank, apply the brakes and attempt to start while moving the selector through the different drive ranges. If maladjusted, the switch may close in one of the drive positions so make this test with caution.

If the engine still fails to crank, touch a battery booster cable momentarily to the battery's positive terminal after connecting the other end to the following points:

General Motors cars—To the solenoid terminal on top of the starter assembly. There are three terminals. The smallest is the proper one for this test.

Chrysler cars—To the solenoid terminal on top of the starter assembly. There are two terminals. Again, the smaller is the right one.

Ford cars—To the starter terminal of the starter relay (the heavy cable from the starter leads directly to the proper relay terminal).

These tests bypass the key-operated starter switch, the neutral safety switch, a relay (on Ford and Chrysler cars) and the interconnecting wiring—all of which make up the starter control circuit.

Thus, if the engine *still* refuses to crank, the starter probably is kaput. Replace it with a new or rebuilt unit after checking the brushes in the original (both are jobs the average weekend mechanic can handle). However, if you happen to discover this while off on

CRANK the engine with coil lead held near a good ground. A strong spark should result.

CHECK the inside of distributor for dust or cracks that mean high-resistance leaks.

a jaunt the only way to get started is to arrange a push.

**If the engine cranks**—If the starter is cranking in healthy fashion all the foregoing checks are superfluous. Instead, you should begin with these quick but proven tests on the ignition and fuel system:

1. Should the engine start but stall immediately when you release the key it proves that the ignition resistor is defective. This resistor is bypassed during cranking so the engine will start. But once the key is released, current must

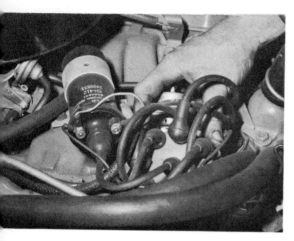

ATTEMPT to move the distributor by hand. If it's loose, ignition timing may be upset.

REMOVE the air filter to check visually that automatic choke opens if engine's hot.

flow through a different circuit, which also includes the resistor. (Note: We're referring to the ignition primary circuit resistor which is put in at the factory, not the radio-suppression type you may have added to the ignition secondary.)

2. Pull the center lead (the one that goes to the coil) from the distributor cap and hold it about a half-in. from electrical ground (any metal part of the engine). Have someone crank the engine for a few seconds. You should see sparks jumping from the end of the wire to ground. If there's no spark move the lead closer to ground. If there's only a weak spark (probably intermittent) proceed directly to step 4. If no one is around to turn the key to crank the engine you can jump the starter switch by connecting one end of a booster cable to the battery and holding the other end against the starter terminal.

3. A healthy, continuous spark from the coil indicates there's spark going into the distributor cap so check next to see that it's being distributed to the plugs.

Disconnect a few spark-plug wires at the plugs—one at a time. Hold each wire a half-in. from ground and again have the engine cranked. The spark should occur less frequently but should be as robust as the discharge from the coil wire. If it is, the ignition system is good. Proceed to step 7.

If the spark is weak or non-existent, remove the distributor cap and check the inside of the cap carefully (use a flashlight), looking for fine cracks or a dirt film that could provide a leakage path for the spark. Clean or replace the cap as necessary.

Inspect the coil and plug lead inserts in the cap for corrosion which could provide a great deal of resistance and weaken the spark. Clean out any corrosion with a wire brush.

4. No spark or a weak spark from the coil could be caused by a poor coil, improperly gapped points, a defective condenser or a broken or loose connection.

Because it's the most likely item, the point gap should be checked first (with the rubbing block at a peak of the cam). It should be somewhat between .012 and .020-in. (the thickness of one business card or something similar).

Next make a quick check of the ignition primary circuit by turning on the ignition and flicking the breaker points open with a screwdriver. You should see a solid electrical arc at the points, which tells you there is a complete circuit from the ignition switch through the coil to the points.

5. If there is little or no arcing connect a thin jumper from the battery's positive terminal to the coil's primary positive terminal (marked with a plus sign, an S or SW). Try the arcing test again. If it works the problem is a poor

or broken connection at the ignition switch, a junction block, a resistor or the coil itself.

Checking back through the circuit imposes some difficulties for the weekend wrench-twirler. But the jumper wire probably will correct any ignition malfunction and get the car running. Then visit your friendly garage. At least you won't get hit with a towing bill.

If the test produces no results, connect a jumper to the other primary terminal of the coil. With the ignition turned on, scratch the other end of this jumper against a ground. You should see heavy sparking as you scratch. No sparks mean current is not flowing through the coil, which must be open at some internal point. Replace the coil.

6. If this last test is successful, current is flowing through the coil but is not getting to the breaker points. Obviously the lead from the coil to the points is open. Replace it.

7. The sparks not only must be healthy but they must arrive at each cylinder at the proper time. Try to move the distributor body. Don't be bashful about using force. If the distributor moves at all under hand pressure, ignition timing may have been upset by engine vibration.

**In checking the fuel system,** remember that only in a few cases will a bad carburetor prevent starting. A malfunctioning automatic choke will do it.

The choke should be closed when the engine is cold, open when it's hot. You can check by removing the air filter and looking.

If the choke is in proper position, check for carburetor flooding. If the carb is flooding badly enough to prevent starting you'll smell the raw fuel through a stiff head cold. You might even get the whiff when you're behind the wheel.

More than likely, however, the fuel isn't getting to the carb. A simple check, with the air filter off, is to open the choke manually so you can see into the carburetor air horn. Yank open the throttle and look for a strong spurt of gasoline into the air horn.

If there's only a dribble, chances are the fuel filter is clogged, the fuel line is

CHECK the battery cable terminals. Make sure they are clean and tight at the battery.

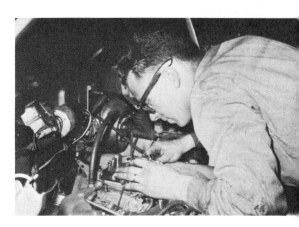

LOOK down carb air horn and yank throttle open to see if fuel is delivered to the carb.

plugged or kinked, or you have a bad fuel pump.

Loosen but don't disconnect the carburetor fuel-line connection at the fuel pump. Crank the engine. If fuel fizzles out the problem is in the line to the carburetor, most likely a clogged filter. If no gasoline comes out the pump is defective.

Under normal conditions it should take less than ten minutes to run the checks we've outlined. For example, if the engine fails to crank, correcting that problem normally will get the car going. Or the engine may crank satisfactorily, permitting you to bypass the series of checks for no cranking. •

BACKING PLATE

ANCHOR PIN

WHEEL CYLINDER

SHOE RETURN SPRING

BRAKE LINING

BRAKE SHOE ASSEMBLY

ADJUSTING SCREW SPRING

ADJUSTING SCREW

# Reline Your Own Brakes

MENTION a do-it-yourself brake job to most drivers and you soon may find yourself wondering if you're suffering from halitosis or B.O. That's how long it will take your audience to remember an important appointment, a Boy Scout meeting, or an April 15th tax deadline.

And yet to those at all acquainted with brakes, the relining process is as simple as ABC. The fact is that anyone can do a first rate job if he uses a methodical approach.

Heading the methodical list, of course, is the question: When will I need a brake job?

**Inspect the brake linings** in a new car after driving about 10,000 miles. Heavy cars subjected to stop-and-go city driving or panic-type stops tend to have a short brake lining life.

Never take the condition of the brake

ON FRONT WHEELS, remove grease cap and cotter pin. Use a box wrench to remove axle nut. Turn counterclockwise to remove.

ON REAR WHEELS, a stuck drum can be removed with the aid of a pair of drum removal tools (bought at little cost) as shown.

AFTER the drum is removed, check the thickness of the linings. These have been saturated in grease and must be replaced.

USE another special tool called brake spring pliers to unhook the heavy pullback springs. Note how they are attached.

linings on a used or second-hand car for granted. Remove a front wheel and inspect. When the useful lining thickness is about $\frac{1}{16}$-in., replace the lining.

Don't wait until the rivets start to cut grooves in the drums, for refacing the brake drum will increase its diameter and reduce its ability to shed heat. If you replace the lining before the drums are damaged it won't be necessary to reface them on a lathe.

**Once you've determined** that a brake job is in order, the next step is the pur-

chase of the replacement linings. There are many brands of replacement linings available through parts houses, dealers and accessory shops. But surprisingly, there is little correlation between price and quality. Your best bet when selecting a set of linings is to rely on well-known brand names.

Before attempting inspection or removal of the lining, make sure that the car won't move. Don't trust the bumper jack. Use a hydraulic or scissors jack wherever possible. If possible, use two

LIFT the shoes away from the backing plate and the star wheel adjuster and spring will separate. Clean and lubricate (see text).

REASSEMBLE the brake mechanism in the following order: secondary shoe, star wheel and spring, bar and finally, primary shoe.

jacks—one under the chassis and the other under the wheel suspension that you're working on. Shake the car after it's raised—it shouldn't budge.

**Whether working on the front** or rear wheels, the first step is to remove the wheel lugs and the tire. On the front wheel, remove the grease cap, cotter pin, nut, washer, outer wheel bearing and drum. Then check the thickness of the linings and the condition of the wheel cylinders, grease seals and drum. If the drums are badly scored, most local parts houses will reface the drums for about a dollar each.

Brake spring pliers are used to remove the pull-back springs, while a pair of ordinary slip-joint pliers will help remove the small springs and pins that hold the shoes against the back plates. The linings, along with the adjusting wheel and its spring, come off next. Clean the back plate thoroughly.

**Disassemble, clean and coat** the threads of the adjusting wheel with Lubriplate. Apply a light smear of Lubriplate where the shoes rub on the backing plate. Reassemble the new lining, the adjusting wheel (screwed together) and its spring. Place them against the backing plate and connect the hold-down pins and clips. Then hook the pull-back spring over the washer to the pin at the top of the backing plate. Check to see if you have any parts left over.

Sand the lining lightly to remove any grease spots. Slip the drum over the axle and replace the wheel bearing with fresh grease. Replace the outer bearing, more grease, washer, nut, cotter pin and the dust cap. Put back the wheel and tighten the wheel nuts on the lugs.

**Finally, the linings** are adjusted with a brake shoe adjuster, often called a *spoon*. Turn the star wheel so that it forces the shoes against the drums. When the wheel can't be rotated, stop. Then back off on the adjusting wheel until the drum turns freely (about eight to ten clicks or notches of the star wheel).

The procedure for the rear wheels is about the same—the only exception being the mechanically operated arm attached to the secondary shoe. It simply is unbolted and attached to the new shoe There's no need to repack rear wheel bearings. Adjust the rear linings as you did for the front.

**Check the foot** or hand-operated emergency brake. It should hold the car securely after being pulled up or stepped down a few notches. If not, an adjustment (shortening) of the hand brake cable must be made by tightening the nuts on the hand brake assembly under the car.

Technically, the brake job is complete, but drive cautiously for a week or two, applying the brakes gently until the linings are seated to the drums. Then readjust the linings on all four wheels if the foot pedal depresses more than an inch or two. •

# Bolt-On Horsepower

IF your car was born with tired blood you can bolt on enough new spirit in an afternoon to outrun almost everything but the drag strip's funny cars.

And if you use the extra scat judiciously, your car will stay out of the repair shop and you'll stay out of jail.

Bringing a tame engine up to satisfying standards with bolt-on equipment is a happy consequence of Detroit's current engine-building technique. A car may be offered with just one V8—say a 400 cubic-incher. That 400 cu. in. may be set up for as little as 250 hp or over 400. So if your version gasps at the sight of a freeway you can bolt on parts—some of which may be factory setups—to get the cubes working a little harder.

The fastest, cheapest way to get the biggest horsepower increase is by supercharging. A moderately supercharged engine, with no great strain, will develop well over 1 hp per cubic inch. A complete kit costs $150 to $250 for small foreign cars and $450 to $900 for American V8s.

A supercharger does exactly what the name says. It forces a king-size charge of air-fuel mixture into the cylinders by use of either a positive-action pump or a fan-like blower. When the engine burns more air-fuel mixture, it produces more power.

The supercharger usually is mounted between carburetor and intake manifold. The popular Judson brand, made for foreign cars and the Corvair only, is the pump type. It provides a power increase starting at low speed and running up through most of the speed range.

The Paxton model, made for a wide variety of American cars, is the centrifugal type, a fan that blows in extra air-fuel mixture. It is most effective at higher engine speeds, when the fan is spinning faster.

The conventional supercharger is driven by a belt off the crankshaft pulley. There are, however, units that are driven by the flow of exhaust gases against a turbine wheel. They are called turbocharges and are available in

MANIFOLD kits are available either from the factory or racing-equipment firms to adapt larger carburetors to engines. This one fits a 4-barrel carb to a Dodge Six. From Offenhauser Sales Corp.

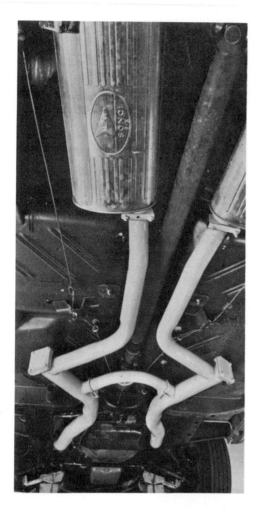

DUAL EXHAUST pipes are standard with hot Dodge engine, can be fitted to others.

limited quantities from small, back-yard companies. Consult your speed shop to see what he can get for you.

**A word of caution.** There was a turbocharger used in 1962 and '63 on Olds F-85s with the 215-cu.-in. aluminum V8. We'll spare you the details about the problems connected with its use and suggest you forget it.

Shelby-American of Los Angeles sells a bolt-on supercharger kit for the 260-289-cu.-in. Ford V8s found in Falcons, Fairlanes and Mustangs. The ads claim it ups horsepower 46% and one hot rod magazine that bought one agrees wholeheartedly.

**The wildest of the lot are** sold by Turbonique, Inc., Orlando, Fla. They are auxiliary-powered superchargers, meaning that the blower is powered by some other source than the car's engine. This sends the power usually needed to turn the supercharger straight to the back wheels, where it does the most good. All of Turbonique's models are demand units. They don't operate all the time, only when you floor the accelerator.

One model is driven by a 4-hp electric motor and has increased the power of an otherwise stock Corvette by 107 hp.

The liquid-fuel model is guaranteed to double your horsepower or you get your money back. When the gas pedal is floored a special liquid fuel is ignited in a small turbine chamber and this turbine runs the supercharger. There is a separate ignition key for the supercharger so your 600-hp Barracuda, for example, won't surprise an unsuspecting parking-lot attendant. The fuel can be any one of several industrial chemicals available from Dow, Olin Mathieson and Union Carbide and from Turbonique. Prices start at $1.35 a gallon, but you don't use that much of it.

**Way out in left field** is a solid-propellant model which operates for ten seconds when you pull a cable under the dash. Then you have to hop out and insert a new solid fuel cartridge.

Turbonique claims that most showroom engines equipped with their devices can safely develop twice normal horsepower (and at normal rpm) for short durations without harm.

But even the smallest superchargers can pose a problem. Because they ram extra air-fuel mixture into the cylinders, they also raise the engine's effective compression ratio. If the engine's compression ratio is about 9:1, it must be lowered before the supercharger can be installed. At the least, a second head gasket will be needed. In some cases, low-compression pistons are the only way—which effectively knocks out supercharging as a bolt-on modification.

**If you buy a supercharger kit,** make sure it includes linkage, mounting hardware and, if applicable, a pulley and drive belt. A new carburetor is some-

UNIQUE supercharger doubles horsepower. It can use a car's normal manifold and carburetor, mounts anywhere there's room under the hood. It operates only when the gas pedal is floored. Turbonique, Inc.

times needed, to the tune of $25 more.

A supercharger does take room in the engine compartment, and therefore will create service headaches. But the well-designed setup will minimize them. Although the supercharger is the fastest way to a big horsepower jump, just remember that it will place an extra strain on the entire drive train.

If you're of a more conservative bent, there are less expensive ways to go. The use of larger carburetion is a simple way to get extra horsepower. The exact power increase will vary widely, according to the design of the cylinder heads and camshaft.

As a general rule, you can get a horsepower increase you'll really feel—at least five per cent—by going one step up in carburetion. For example, if your car has a V8 with a two-barrel, go to a four-barrel. If it has a four-barrel, change to three two-barrels or two four-barrels.

**Even a six-cylinder engine** can take extra carburetion. A larger one-barrel, or a two-barrel, plus a well-designed intake manifold can add a fast six to ten hp.

Never try to go hog-wild with carburetion alone. If you've got a two-bar-

rel on that V8, going to two four-barrels is a waste of money if it isn't accompanied by substantial internal modifications. Without them, the engine can easily end up over-carbureted: gas velocities drop, spark plugs foul, the engine develops flat spots and often floods at low speed.

The simplest procedure is to bolt on a factory setup. That is, just buy the factory's optional intake manifold and carburetor for your particular engine. If you buy used parts from a wrecking yard, the cost probably won't exceed $40. If you don't it could hit $100. The wrecking yard also is a good place to visit for non-factory performance parts. There are wreckers who specialize in them, and the savings over the new prices are impressive. Just make sure you get a complete linkage setup. Cobbling something to fit is not fun; nor is it fast or cheap.

**If you've improved the intake** system, either by supercharging or adding carburetion, you should do something to enable the exhaust system to handle the increased flow of gases.

If the exhaust system is restricted, burned gases can't escape fast enough and pressure backs up to the cylinder, reducing most of the power gained by the improved intake, particularly at high speed. But you don't have to go to extremes.

Merely going up one step in carburetion doesn't require a complete exhaust system overhaul. A freer breathing muffler and tailpipe usually are enough and you can obtain them for approximately the same price as standard units (perhaps 10 to 15 per cent higher) from most speed shops. Fiberglass-packed mufflers are very low in restriction, even lower in price than standard units and will usually provide a maximum increase in breathability. But they are somewhat noisy and illegal in some states.

If you supercharge a V8, you should go to a free-breathing dual exhaust. If you have a standard dual exhaust to start with, just change mufflers and resonators and the improvement should be adequate.

After these changes, horsepower increases come far more slowly and at considerably greater cost. Anything else in the bolt-on category is going to be tied to another improvement that isn't. For example, installing a dual-breaker-point distributor or transistor ignition is going to keep the spark hot at very high engine speed. But unless your engine is internally modified for high speed, the benefits of the distributor may be nonexistent.

**Relatively large power increases** still are possible, but they involve at least partial dismantling of the engine for new pistons, camshaft and crankshaft, machining of the cylinder heads, and other very expensive work.

You can spend thousands of dollars adding horsepower in many ways. But unless you're going to put your rig on the track, you can bolt on all you will ever be able to use. •

CONVENTIONAL supercharger is run by belts from the crankshaft, operates all the time. Kits are sold to adapt them to most medium-size American engines and some foreign models. From Judson Research & Mfg. Co.

# When Your Water Pump Doesn't Pump

THERE'S nothing on a modern automobile's water pump to adjust. You needn't clean it and you can barely disassemble it without special tools. So it would seem that the water pump is something to forget about until it gives trouble.

This would be a mistake. There are several things the weekend mechanic can do that will determine water pump life. And unless he replaces a defective unit correctly he'll have another pump failure in short order.

**The operation of the pump** is nothing complicated in itself. Both the crankshaft and the water pump have pulleys connected by a rubber belt, which usually wraps around the generator pulley as well. The fan blades are attached to the front of the water-pump pulley. At the back end of the pump's shaft is a circular member with vanes called the impeller—which is the heart of the pump.

The impeller, made of plastic or cast iron, is spun by the shaft and scoops up hot water from the pump inlet, forcing it through an outlet pipe to the radiator. The water flow between pump and radiator is controlled by the thermostat. When the 'stat is open, water is pumped through to the radiator at a rate that may reach 125 gallons per minute. When the 'stat is closed, as during warmup, a small hole in the pump allows the water to bypass the radiator.

**Now, let's look at some** construction details. The impeller is press-fitted on the shaft and bears against a spring-loaded seal assembly, which sits in a recess in the pump cavity. Minor wear, caused by the impeller spinning against the face of the seal, is compensated for by the thickness of the seal and outward pressure of the seal-assembly's spring.

The shaft is supported in a bearing assembly at the front of the pump. Ball bearings are standard, although plain shell types have been used.

The water-pump case is either cast iron or aluminum, with aluminum most common on late-model cars (it's cheaper).

**Let's see what can go wrong.** That

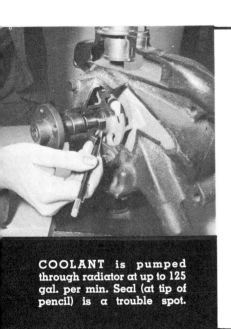

**COOLANT is pumped through radiator at up to 125 gal. per min. Seal (at tip of pencil) is a trouble spot.**

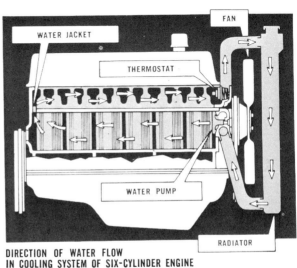

DIRECTION OF WATER FLOW
IN COOLING SYSTEM OF SIX-CYLINDER ENGINE

spring-loaded seal assembly can wear enough so eventually it will start to leak and, in fact, most water pumps are replaced because of leakage at the seal.

But many a good pump is blamed for leakage. The pump should not leak continuously when the engine is either stopped or rotating, but if the engine has not been run for a couple of months give the pump seal at least 30 minutes of engine operation to reform.

And, of course, be sure that you know where the leak is coming from. If the seal is bad the leak should be through a small vent hole in the pump. A leak from any other point may indicate a crack in the pump housing but could also be something as simple as a defective gasket or a loose nut.

Normally the pump seal assembly will perform satisfactorily for the life of the car. It's a special graphite-impregnated plastic, helped in part by a lubricant in antifreeze and rust inhibitors. When the seal fails the reason usually is premature wear caused by abrasive particles in the cooling system.

**If you want to avoid** an even earlier failure with the replacement pump, drain and flush the cooling system with the old leaking pump still in place. This is a good idea, no matter what caused

the pump to fail, because you're going to have to drain the cooling system, anyway.

If you're in a hard-water area you may have special problems. Hard water contains minerals that will leave deposits that flake off and damage the pump. Get some soft water somehow (buy it from a laundromat if you must), or give the cooling system a good flush with a chemical cleaner at least once a year.

If you haven't a hard-water problem, your best bet is to use a high-quality antifreeze (one of the big name brands) and drain it each fall. Good antifreeze has sufficient corrosion inhibitor and water-pump lubricant to last a year (and the antifreezing quality never wears out as it did in the old days).

If you've already poured in some 90 cents-a-gallon antifreeze, drain it at the first opportunity and buy something good. It's a lot cheaper than the price of a spring flush and can of inhibitor.

Although water leaking past the seal is a common cause of pump bearing failure, there is a companion that's also quite popular: excessive tightening of the fan belt. A tight belt puts tremendous stress on the bearings. So if you're built like King Kong or do your belt

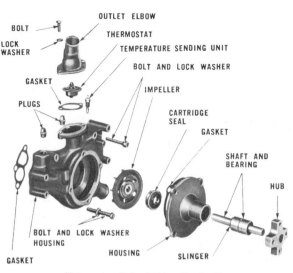

BOLT
LOCK WASHER
GASKET
PLUGS
OUTLET ELBOW
THERMOSTAT
TEMPERATURE SENDING UNIT
BOLT AND LOCK WASHER
IMPELLER
CARTRIDGE SEAL
GASKET
SHAFT AND BEARING
HUB
BOLT AND LOCK WASHER
HOUSING
GASKET
HOUSING
SLINGER

Photo courtesy Dodge Division, Chrysler Motors

IMPELLER is the heart of the pump. The one above leaked due to scoring by abrasive coolant particles.

adjustments with a crowbar, watch out.

A narrow belt should deflect a half-inch when moderate finger pressure is applied between water pump and generator pulleys (a wide belt can deflect a full inch). If the belt deflects noticeably more, it's too loose and will slip on the pulley. The pump won't turn fast enough and the engine may overheat. If it deflects less it's too tight.

**Before replacing a pump** because of allegedly defective bearings, make sure that you've diagnosed the trouble correctly. Take off the belt and try to move the pump shaft from side to side. If you can feel shaft move, bearings are worn.

Don't decide the bearings are shot by engine-compartment noise. Spray some brake fluid on the belt to eliminate the possibility of belt noise fooling your ear (and be sure the belt is adjusted properly). Make certain that the noise is metallic and that it's coming from the water pump.

A currently-important cause of water-pump problems is cavitation and the erosion it causes. Cooling system passageways restricted by corrosion result in reduced water pressure at the pump. Because of the lower pressure, the water vaporizes. As the vapor moves through the pump, it again becomes pressurized and bursts into water bubbles. The vaporization-and-bubbling sequence is called cavitation.

These bubbles collapse against the metal surfaces of the pump, creating shock waves with pressures

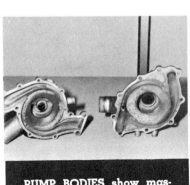

**PUMP BODIES show massive erosion created by cavitation. Restricted water passages can lead to cavitation.**

as high as 200,000 psi. The bursting bubbles dig little particles out of the pump body and impeller. The displaced particles may cause some damage on their own but, equally important, they increase the size of the interior of the pump and the total effect is to decrease pump output.

As the engine ages and deposits build up and reduce the ability of the coolant to conduct heat, erosion of the water pump occurs. Combined with other causes, an older car obviously is more likely to overheat.

**Installing a water pump** is well within the ability of the weekend mechanic. To gain working clearance, it's usually necessary to pull the radiator but this is a matter of four to eight bolts on most cars.

You have the choice of a new or rebuilt pump. Kits are available for rebuilding pumps but the job requires an arbor press and other items not normally found in the weekend mechanic's toolbox. New pumps range from $8 to $25; rebuilts a bit more than half price.

**Start the job** by flushing the cooling system, then drain. Pull the radiator and undo the bolts that hold the water pump in place. Remove the pump and scrape away all traces of gasket from the block.

If the pump is aluminum and the gasket thin paper, coat both sides of the gasket with sealer.

Handle the pump carefully. Dropping it can bend a shaft or flatten a bearing, which will be enough to shorten its life. Once the pump is in place, gradually tighten all bolts as evenly as you can.

Trying out the pump without water in the engine can damage the seal. Refill the cooling system, let the engine warm up until the thermostat is open and then remove the radiator cap to check for coolant circulation.

Stand at one side of the engine, and with it running at 2,000 rpm or so, watch the pulley and fan assembly for wobble. Crooked pulleys or bent fan blades can cause the pump to be out of balance at high speeds, a condition that will cause premature shaft or bearing failure. •

# THE _NEW_ STORY ON

# TAPPETS!

TELL the average week-end mechanic that his hydraulic tappets
may need adjusting and he'll give you
that don't-be-stupid stare.

"Hydraulic tappets were designed to
replace mechanical tappets and don't
need adjustment," he'll tell you flatly.

For those who know the headache of
clattering fluid tappets there's no such
reaction. Many also have discovered
that if valves have been ground, the
cylinder head removed or a lifter or
two replaced, adjustments are almost
certain to be needed. But even these
more experienced folk may not realize
that some of the techniques applied to
silencing mechanical tappets can be a
real help in silencing the latter-day fluid
variety.

**Just in case** you haven't spent much
time around automobile engines or
reading the pages of car-service manuals, tappets go by several names. By
definition they are cam followers. They
also are valve lifters.

The valves of the engine are operated
by the camshaft through the valve train.
In the most common layout today, the
overhead-valve engine, the tappet or
valve lifter rides its respective cam; a
push rod extending from the lifter connects to a rocker arm, and the opposite
arm of the rocker contacts the tip of the
valve stem. The valve itself is held on
its seat by a coil spring. It is the spring
which forces the tappet to follow the
profile of the cam lobe.

**With mechanical** (or solid) tappets,
the most common adjustment is for
valve lash or clearance between the
rocker arm and valve stem. This is
known rather loosely as tappet adjustment.

Too little clearance between the tip
of the rocker arm and the valve stem
will cause valve burning. Too much will
cause the valve to be hammered by the
cam. Since solid lifters can't adjust
themselves for normal wear, most engines with mechanical tappets are fitted
with lash-adjusting screws and lock
nuts. Adjustment can be made with a
wrench, a screwdriver and a flat feeler
gauge.

**In theory,** fluid lifters provide a cush-
ion of oil to absorb operating shocks and
to serve as an automatic adjustment
medium which maintains zero lash in
the valve-operating linkage under all
operating conditions. When these lifters
are set up after a motor job, however,
there has to be a certain amount of
valve lash between the stem and rocker
arm when the lifter is collapsed and
while on the heel of the cam. If the gap
is less than the minimum specified the
valve probably has been ground down
too far and should be replaced. If the
gap is more than the maximum allowed
the valve face should be ground down

Buick valve mechanism.

further. This applies to the so-called nonadjustable hydraulic lifter.

In the case of adjustable fluid lifters you'll know when the end clearance is removed simply by moving the push rod with your fingers as the stud nut is tightened. By applying pressure slowly on the push rod you can bleed down the lifter until the plunger bottoms. Hold the lifter in this collapsed position while checking the clearance. Turn the rocker-arm stud nut clockwise to decrease lash, counterclockwise to increase it.

**The correct position** for the crankshaft when checking any one set of tappets is obtained by cranking until the piston for that cylinder is at top dead center. You also have guidance markings on the vibration damper at the front end of the engine. Easiest way to turn over the engine slowly is to remove the spark plugs and pull on the fan belt.

But before digging into details of hydraulic lifter servicing let's take a look at the silencing of mechanical lifters or what passes for silence.

**A common mistake** is to try to overcome a single tap or two by quieting all of the lifters. It is far better to leave a little more clearance all around so as to get a rhythmic noise rather than one or two disturbing knocks.

REMOVE rocker-arm cover, strip off old gasket and scrape up deposits of sludge.

VALVE LASH is best adjusted with engine running. Use wrench and flat feeler gauge.

Valve lash in some instances may be the same for intake valves as for exhausts but usually there's more clearance for exhausts because of the greater anticipated expansion of these valves from superheated exhaust gases. You usually find a greater difference with high-performance engines but this isn't always the measuring stick. The Plymouth 1966 Six, for instance, requires

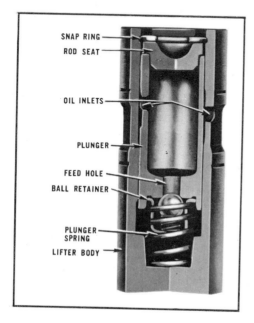

SNAP RING
ROD SEAT
OIL INLETS
PLUNGER
FEED HOLE
BALL RETAINER
PLUNGER SPRING
LIFTER BODY

.010 in. for intakes and .020 in. for exhausts, *checked when the engine is hot.*

**For adjusting** mechanical tappets on an L-head engine you need a flat feeler gauge and two wrenches. One wrench is used to adjust for clearance; the other turns the locking nut. Mechanics who have been around a while prefer to adjust with the engine warmed up—at least ten minutes driving on the road—and idling.

The adjusting screw is turned in or out until the feeler of the thickness corresponding to the clearance specs can just be moved between the screw and valve stem. Then tighten the locking nut.

On an overhead-valve engine the adjustment is made by loosening the lock nut with a wrench and turning the adjusting screw with a screwdriver. The

feeler gauge slips between the rocker arm and the valve stem—also with engine idling.

**Badly worn** or scuffed valve tips and rocker-arm pads or off-square rocker-arm pads also may cause noise at idle that becomes louder as engine speed is increased. Sometimes this can be eliminated by rotating the valve spring and valve. Check also for excessive valve-stem-to-guide clearance.

There are important details for various engines so get all the facts about your own car before tackling even what may seem to be a routine job. For example, on 1961-1964 Ford engines silent valve lash is achieved with mechanical tappets by using a rocker-arm eccentric to compensate for wear on the valve train.

**With hydraulic lifters,** engine oil, oil pressure and cleanliness are important factors. Tapping from a single lifter invariably is a sign that there is dirt in it. Air in the oiling system can produce lifter noise but a general clatter is the result rather than an isolated tap. Too-light oil or oil that breaks down under high bearing pressure or high engine temperature will cause general lifter clatter. That explains why a compact's engine may sound like a truck's when you mistake the pike for the Indianapolis Speedway and then quiet to a purr when you remember the local constabulary's speed trap.

Looking into a fluid lifter, we find that it is merely a plunger in a cylinder. In the closed position of the check valve at the bottom oil is trapped in the compression chamber. Thus the lift of the cam is transmitted to the plunger and the lifter body to open the corresponding engine poppet valve. Then, as the camshaft turns farther, the valve spring for this particular valve assembly forces the lifter down to reseat the valve. The lifter's plunger spring pushes the plunger upward so as to draw oil through an opened check valve into the compression chamber. Oil is fed to all lifters through galleries in the crankcase.

**Adjust hydraulic lifters** for zero lash with the engine warm and running at idle. Back off the rocker-arm nut until the valve rocker arm starts to clatter, then turn the rocker-arm nut down slowly until the clatter just stops. This is the zero lash position. Turn the nut down ¼ additional turn and pause ten seconds until the engine runs smoothly. Repeat additional quarter turns, pausing ten seconds each time, until the nut has been turned down the one or 1½ turns specified from the zero-lash position.

This preload adjustment must be done slowly to allow the lifter to adjust itself and prevent the possibility of interference which might result in internal damage. Bulged tappet bodies, bent push rods and permanently noisy operation may result if the tappets are forced down too rapidly.

**Whether tappets** are solid or fluid, be sure to consider that the valves themselves may be the source of the noise. If there is stickage you may be able to cure it easily by using tune-up oil in the gasoline. But you have to be persistent. Sometimes a valve won't move up and down easily in its guide unless it has the continuous benefit of solvents fed to it via the gas mixture.

And a lot of valve-train noise comes from wear and tear on the rocker arms. This, in turn, may be due to lube starvation. Sludge and gums form in the area and clog oil passages. It pays to take off valve covers occasionally and remove sludge.

When replacing valve covers take care not to overtighten them. You are likely to amplify valve noise. And you may cause the covers to buckle. That will make it harder for the cover gaskets to seal; oil will leak out and run down the rear of the engine. It may result in the mechanism having too little oil when the engine is started after a lay-up of a week or so.

**There's no use** getting excited if tappets clatter a bit when the engine is cold. Oil may drain from the lifters which are holding the valves open when the engine is not running. It takes a few seconds for these lifters to fill after the engine is started. My old Packard V-12 used to sound like the Jolly Green Giant's marbles clicking on a hardwood floor. But that was considered standard.

Today we normally have little leakdown of oil from the lifters and such fast pressure build-up that there is no lifter clatter at all with many engines. But if there is clatter it should disappear quickly as the engine warms up.

The noise level of the valve train cannot be judged properly when the engine is below operating temperature, when the hood is raised or when rocker-arm covers are removed. Make your check from the driver's seat, running the engine at idle speed, then at various higher speeds.

**The oil level** in the pan never should be above the full mark on the dipstick nor below the add-oil mark. Either of these two conditions could be responsible for noisy tappets.

If the oil level is above full it is possible for the connecting rods to dip into oil while the engine is running and create foam. Foam in the oil pan would be fed to the hydraulic tappets by the oil pump, causing them to go flat and allowing the valves to seat noisily.

Low oil level may allow the pump to take in air which, when fed to the tappets, causes them to lose length and allows the valves to seat noisily.

Water in the oil also will cause clatter.

**Let's consider** the problem of a single tappet beating out a tribal tune. Maybe the trouble is due to a weak or broken plunger spring in the troublesome lifter. The plunger may be worn or too tight in the lifter body. The ball valve may leak.

You can locate a leak-down condition by putting your finger on the valve-spring retainer while the engine idles. The cushioning action of the lifter will be lessened if there's too much leak-down and you'll feel a sharp knock as the valve seats. It's best to replace lifters which show high leak-down.

**To pick out** the abnormally noisy tappet place one end of a four-ft. length of garden hose or heater hose near each valve in turn and listen through the other end of hose.

If you find carbon, dirt or varnish in one tappet, chances are you'll find it in all of them. But always remove and replace tappets one at a time. *They are not interchangeable.* Car makers stress that mixed parts won't work here. •

# Servicing Power Brakes

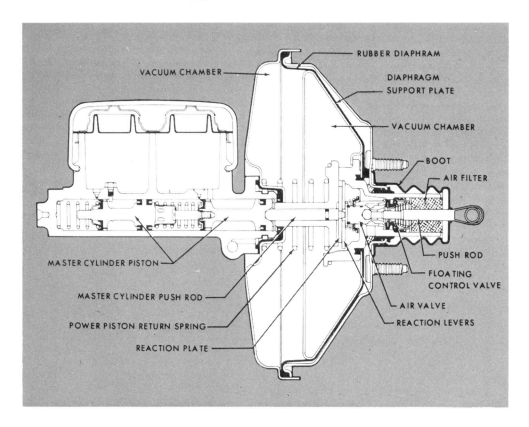

RUBBER DIAPHRAM

DIAPHRAGM
SUPPORT PLATE

VACUUM CHAMBER

VACUUM CHAMBER

BOOT

AIR FILTER

PUSH ROD

FLOATING
CONTROL VALVE

AIR VALVE

REACTION LEVERS

MASTER CYLINDER PISTON

MASTER CYLINDER PUSH ROD

POWER PISTON RETURN SPRING

REACTION PLATE

TO BLEED master cylinder remove brake line while someone floors pedal. Cover opening with thumb when brake is released.

POWER accessories are the last thing a weekend mechanic attempts to fix. Although it's good to recognize things you are not equipped to handle, there are many parts of the power steering and braking systems that parallel those in non-power systems.

Many different power brake units are made for passenger cars. All use engine vacuum to boost the braking force supplied by your foot. The units are designed so that, should the power fail, you can stop anyway, although some early models require quite a bit of foot pressure.

When the brake pedal is pushed, a valve in the power unit lets engine intake vacuum suck air out of a chamber on one side of a diaphragm, bellows or

# and Power Steering

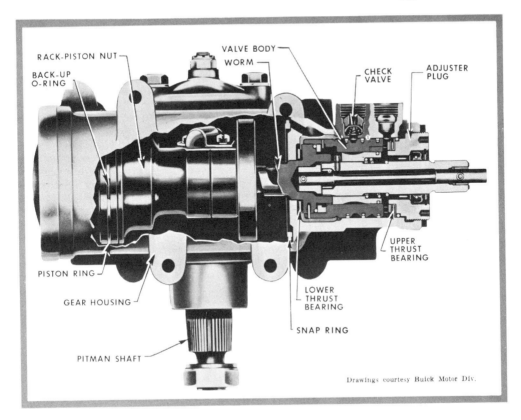

RACK-PISTON NUT
BACK-UP O-RING
VALVE BODY
WORM
CHECK VALVE
ADJUSTER PLUG
PISTON RING
GEAR HOUSING
UPPER THRUST BEARING
LOWER THRUST BEARING
SNAP RING
PITMAN SHAFT

Drawings courtesy Buick Motor Div.

piston. Atmospheric pressure pushing on the other side gives the master cylinder's piston a boost, building up hydraulic pressure in the braking system. You supply a little of the effort and the power booster supplies the rest. Except for the booster unit, the parts of a power brake system are like those of conventional brakes.

A power brake assembly consists of the power booster and a master cylinder. A vacuum hose leads from the intake manifold to the power booster and a hydraulic line (or lines in the case of dual-braking systems) leads to the car's wheel cylinders. Some power brake units have a vacuum reservoir between the power unit and intake manifold. This stores up enough vacuum to make several power-assisted stops without the engine running. All vacuum

**EXAMINE** power steering cylinder shaft for scoring which causes leaks. Some shafts are covered with protective boots.

95

systems have a check valve to keep vacuum in the unit at its peak point for maximum braking assistance.

Most units today are the self-contained type. The master cylinder on these is pretty much like a conventional one except that its piston is extended to receive the actuating rod from the power booster unit.

Finding the trouble in a power brake system is the same as for a non-power system until it is narrowed down to the power unit. Always check the regular brake system first, then the power unit. If the power booster fails to work, the pedal will seem hard.

**To test your power brakes,** apply them several times with the engine off to use up all remaining vacuum inside the power booster. Then apply and hold the brake firmly. Start the engine. The brake pedal should drop slightly but then should stay firm without further travel or sponginess.

If the brake pedal does not fall away, check the vacuum hose and its connections.

If the pedal continues to fall, check and tighten all hydraulic connections and bleed screws. If the pedal still falls when the test is repeated and no fluid leakage is visible, there may be an internal leak in the master cylinder.

If the pedal is spongy, bleed the trapped air out of the hydraulic system.

Release the brake pedal and run the engine a full minute at idle. Then shut it off. After waiting another minute, step on the brake pedal several times. The pedal should become harder each time the brakes are applied. Otherwise there is a vacuum leak.

**If the check valve** in the power booster system is a separate unit (usually located at the intake manifold), disconnect the vacuum hose from the unit. Cover the hose end with your finger and have someone start the engine to create vacuum. Then shut it off. *Vacuum should hold for at least a minute.* If not, the check valve is defective and should be replaced. If the power

booster unit has an internal check valve, you can't make this test.

Check all vacuum hoses for softness or collapsed sides and replace defective ones. Tighten all connections. Inspect the manifold vacuum fitting to make sure it is clear.

Have someone hold the brake pedal down while the engine is running. Listen for a vacuum leak in the unit. A steady hissing is what you're listening for. Try to locate the source of the noise. If it's coming from inside the power booster, you'll have to abandon the rest of the job to a shop. But you can replace or tighten a leaking vacuum hose or connection yourself.

**A power brake that won't** release properly when you let off on the pedal may be suffering from a poorly aligned connection between power unit and brake linkage. If the misaligned connection is inside the power unit, take it to a shop for fixing.

If the power booster is not doing its share of the braking work and everything else seems to be okay, check engine vacuum. If the vacuum is too low—less than 14 in. at idle—tune up the engine to raise its vacuum.

Other maintenance tips on power brakes are pretty conventional: Power brakes are more dependent on brake fluid than conventional ones, so use the best. If the unit has an air filter that you can get at, keep it clean. Maintain brake pedal free play the same as for a conventional system. If the brake pedal must be pushed down more than half its total travel distance, the brake linings need adjustment or replacement.

Heavy front ends and wider tires with lower pressures all have increased steering effort in today's cars to the point where power steering is no longer a luxury.

**Power steering is really** a hydraulic booster arrangement that supplies most of the turning effort when you move the steering wheel. The system consists of an engine-driven pump that supplies hydraulic pressure to the power steering unit. Even if power steering fails, the car can be steered conventionally.

The hydraulic pump is usually belt-driven, but may run off the back of the generator. Using type-A automatic transmission fluid, the pump delivers some 1000 psi. pressure to power unit. A reservoir on pump holds fluid. A filter reservoir keeps the fluid clean.

**There isn't much you can do** on a power steering system. You can check the fluid level at regular intervals and add type-A transmission fluid if necessary. If the level should get too low, the pump begins sucking air and you may have to bleed the system after topping it off. To do this idle the engine while turning the steering wheel rapidly all the way to one side then the other. Roll the front wheels onto several sheets of newspaper first to prevent scuffing the tires and straining the steering system. If there was much air in the system, you'll have to add more fluid.

Keep watch for fluid leaks on the pavement under the front of your car. Sometimes automatic transmission sealants will stop the leaking for a time. Later you'll need professional repairs.

A leak may simply be from an opening in the gasket between the fluid reservoir and its cover. This lets fluid out until there isn't enough left to make a full turn. The pump growls and you have to provide all the turning effort beyond the emptying point. Replace the gasket, refill with fluid and bleed off trapped air.

**To find where fluid is leaking,** wipe off all the power steering system parts and turn the steering wheel from side to side several times with the engine idling. Hold the wheel against the lock each way for a short time to build pressure. Then crawl underneath and inspect for leaks. Even if it turns out to be more than you can fix yourself, helping your mechanic to narrow down the trouble should save you money.

Often a leak is in the shaft seal on the pump. Replacing that and overhauling the pump is not very costly. In fact you can buy a rebuilt pump for $20 to $25 and install it yourself.

If it's a hose that's leaking, a new one costs $6 to $10 complete with end fittings and a tool to install it. Your shop can replace leaky seals in a power cylinder for $8 to $10. A scored piston rod calls for replacement of the entire power cylinder, a $40 to $50 job.

When the trouble is in the control valve or power unit itself, take your car to the shop. Sometimes a simple adjustment is all that's necessary. Other times the unit may need a complete overhaul.

**Before putting the blame** on power steering, the entire steering system, the suspension and wheel alignment should be checked. Front tire pressure that is too low can also be the source of steering difficulties.

Keep a careful check on the pump belt tension. A belt that's loose will squeal every time the steering meets resistance. Too tight a belt can wear out the pump bearings before their time. See that the belt is not glazed, cracked or worn excessively. If it is, replace it. To do this you may have to remove all the belts. Replace them all too.

**On newer cars** belt tension must be checked with a belt tension gauge. If you don't have one, take your car to the shop for this part of the checkup. If bad, you can adjust or replace them.

Here are some power steering problems other than leaks which indicate that professional service is needed: (1) Hard or erratic steering. (2) Excessive play or looseness in steering. (3) Noises in pump (slight hissing sound okay). (4) Lack of assist in one or both directions. (5) Steering wheel surges or jerks when turning. (6) Poor return of steering gear to center. (7) Car pulls to one side. (8) Momentary increase in effort when turning wheel fast. (9) Squawk when turning or recovering from turn. (10) No effort required to turn.

Don't tamper with any part of a car still under warranty as "unauthorized repair" may void the entire contract. •

# Do You Want to Sell Your Car?

COMES a time in every man's life when he has to turn in his old buggy for Detroit's latest. But unless you *think* before selling, you'll never get the best possible price for your car.

Yup, that's really all a wise seller needs to do—*think*. And, incidentally, spend a couple of bucks to dress up the worn machine.

Begin the ponderous thought processes by placing yourself in the buyer's shoes. Examine the car inside and out—then ask yourself how many little things would make *you* shy away if you were the buyer?

Worn pedal pads, for example, spell high mileage. Replacements cost only pennies but get them a couple of weeks before you sell the car to give them a chance to scuff slightly. Brand-new pads will arouse a buyer's suspicions. The same goes for torn floor matting. Replace it ahead of time and let the new matting get some use.

Also watch that telltale left front window-sill molding. Paint worn off means the driver's elbow has been resting there for many miles. Unscrew the molding and spray it with aerosol paint (it's best to spray all four moldings so they match). If the molding is chromed and the plating is worn off, buy a new molding.

**A clean finish** is a must. By all means wash the car and, if the paint is faded, polish it with rubbing compound. A simple wax job can add $50-$75 to the price you'll get for your car.

Even the prospective buyer who can't tell a camshaft from a carburetor knows enough to check under the hood. A greasy engine could kill the sale. Steam-cleaning an engine is expensive and some mechanics feel that hot steam damages wiring and other delicate parts. Instead, buy a quart of kerosene and, with the engine shut off, slosh it on liberally with a well-worn paint brush. Kerosene isn't highly combustible but if your engine is hot wait a few minutes before applying or the kerosene will steam off before it can penetrate the dirt. Just to play safe, disconnect the battery terminals to prevent sparking.

Let the kerosene soak in ten minutes or longer. Then cover the distributor

WORN pedal pads tell tale of high mileage. Replacements cost pennies, snap in place.

GREASY engine is almost certain to kill a sale. Clean it with kerosene and a brush.

cap with a waxed bread wrapper, plastic dry-cleaning bag or other waterproof material to keep the ignition dry. Then wash off the kerosene and sludge with a water hose. Wipe dry with a cloth.

A clean battery is another sign of a careful owner. White acid deposits may resist wire brushing but a tablespoon of ordinary baking soda dissolved in a cup of water will do the trick without scrubbing. Pour the solution over the deposits and wait a few minutes. As the soda bubbles and froths, it neutralizes and loosens the acid deposits so they can be washed off with water. Be careful not to spill the soda solution down the breather holes in the battery caps. If the battery is badly corroded cover the holes with bits of tape so you can pour with abandon.

**The trunk is another area** that's often forgotten by the seller—but not by the buyer. "I can always tell," says one used-car salesman, "what kind of treatment a car's had by the condition of the trunk. If it's neat and clean, it's a safe bet that the rest of the car has had tender loving care."

First clear out any unnecessary clut-

ter that has accumulated over the years. Clean out sand and dirt with a wet rag or heavy-duty vacuum. Wash off the spare wheel and tire. If an interior trunk panel is damaged or missing, repair or replace it. Also check the glove compartment and ash trays, making sure they're clean.

If you are selling to a car dealer, this is as far as you should go with your reconditioning. The dealer can make any further repairs at much less cost than you can.

**If you're selling privately,** repairing any tears in the upholstery is worthwhile, even though it's usually not a do-it-yourself job.

"Even if we show a customer a cream-puff," says one dealer, "if there's a tear in the upholstery, right away he thinks the car's beat up. Maybe there was just a dog jumping around inside but all the buyer is thinking is *high mileage.*"

He advises having an insert (made of factory material) sewn in if it's a late-model car—no more than three years old. With older cars, damage can be covered up with slip covers.

On the other hand, most salesmen

agree that body damage usually isn't worth repairing unless it's a nearly new car in excellent condition. Even then, repairing minor bumps may not pay. One salesman pointed to a late-model Plymouth, flawless except for a small crease in one door. "I could get that fixed for next to nothing," he said, "but I won't. No matter how good a job the body man does, he won't match the paint exactly. If a customer sees that a door has been sprayed, he'll think the car was in a bad wreck. If left un-

sprayed he knows what he's getting."

Bumpers are an exception to the no-fix rule. A beat or dented bumper can be straightened and rechromed to look like new for about a third of the new retail price.

Dealers also agree that complete repainting is almost always a waste of money. If it's an older car you won't get back the price of the paint job. And if it's a late model the buyer will wonder what happened to it to make it need a repainting.

INVESTMENT in body work isn't recommended but do replace lens, polish bumper.

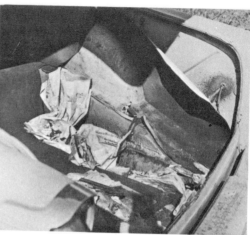

WOULD you buy a car with a trunk like this? Some time, glue and it could look like new.

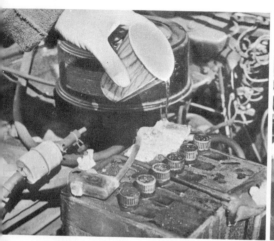

BATTERY connections should be cleaned with teaspoonful of baking soda in water.

AN OWNER too lazy to empty ash tray may have been too lazy to service car regularly.

**It does pay, however,** to touch up tiny chips and scratches by hand. Buy a can of original factory paint and apply with a small artist's brush. Some colors are available in special applicator bottles complete with brushes. The aerosol cans are a bad bet—even an expert may have trouble matching the finish.

When it comes to mechanical repairs, here's another good rule of thumb: Don't invest any money unless the car is making great clanking noises or not running at all.

**Brakes and steering** usually are expensive to repair so it doesn't pay to do anything in those areas unless it's a late model. But for the sake of your conscience, warn a prospective buyer if either of these systems needs work.

Broken side windows are relatively inexpensive to replace but the windshield or rear window should be left for the next owner to take care of. New tires also don't pay. On an older car four new tires may be worth more than the car itself and on a late model they immediately indicate high mileage or rough usage.

Evidence of regular maintenance is one of the most important selling points. Before you put up a car for sale, grease the chassis (if it needs it) and change the oil. Even a buyer who's not mechanically inclined may pull the dipstick. And make sure you get a current service sticker in the door jamb. Few things can sour a sale faster than an old sticker that shows the oil hasn't been changed in the last 10,000 miles.

**When is the best time** to sell your car? If you need money quickly you may have no choice. But if you're in no hurry, pick your time carefully. When the economy is healthy and people are in a buying mood you'll sell your car faster and for more money.

Generally, spring is the best time to sell. One dealer waxed poetic: "In the spring the trees turn green and people who've been hibernating for four or five months suddenly get the urge to travel."

Now the question: *to whom should you sell?* Used-car dealers, of course, are lavish in their descriptions of the advantages of selling to a dealer. And they have some valid points. You get cash immediately. You don't need to put up with cranks who have nothing better to do than take up your time. You don't have to let a lot of strangers test-drive your car or sit home week ends waiting for phone calls. But they readily admit you can get more money through a private sale.

If you try selling privately, first use any available free advertising. The most obvious—and most overlooked—is a for-sale sign in your car window, especially effective if you often park on busy streets. Tell your friends. Put up notices on club, school and other bulletin boards.

If this doesn't work, try a newspaper classified ad. Take advantage of special rates. Often you can get a full week's listing for the same price as two or three days' worth. If you buy an ad by the day, however, remember that Fridays through Sundays are best in the wintertime. That's when most people are free to check the ads and shop. But in the summer everyone is away on week ends so try to advertise on weekdays.

**If the price** you're asking is attractive, mention it in the ad. And take a cue from the dealers—ask for more than you expect so the customer feels he's getting a bargain when he gets the car for less.

To find out what your car is worth, check book prices. Such books are available at most libraries and bookstores. Or check the classified ads and find out what your model is going for.

After you've calculated an average selling price for your model, add to or subtract from this figure according to the car's condition. You can add for such equipment as air conditioning, automatic transmission and power steering and brakes. But don't expect to get more for other extras.

If you decide to sell to a dealer, shop all the lots you can. You're bound to get a wide range of offers. As one dealer put it, "If we're selling lots of cars, we'll pay top price. But if we have five cars of a particular model and you come along with a sixth, you'll do much better taking your car to the lot down the road." •

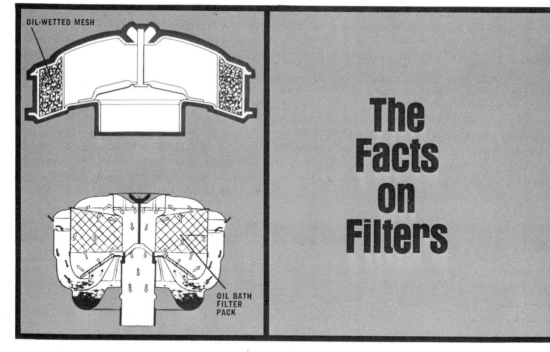

OIL-WETTED MESH

OIL BATH FILTER PACK

# The Facts on Filters

AIR CLEANER on top is often found in sports cars. It traps dirt in oil-soaked mesh. Oil bath model (bottom) holds more dirt than type above, is used chiefly on off-the-road trucks.

IN the Dark Ages, men thought the whole world was made of combinations of four basic elements: water, earth, air and fire. Although we know better now, your car's engine has a series of filters that attempt to keep the first two materials out of the last two. The way some people maintain these filters, you would think it was still the 12th century. Any service station man will tell you they are the most neglected parts in a car.

Yet, if you can turn a wrench, you can service your own oil filter, carburetor air cleaner, fuel filter and crankcase breather vent. Some filter elements can be cleaned and reused indefinitely. And replacement cartridges, where necessary, are quite cheap.

But far too few motorists realize how much damage dirty, clogged filters can do. Let's review the job of each filter and how to maintain it:

**The oil filter,** of course, filters the oil. It keeps metal shavings, carbon and dirt from being ground into engine bearings and moving parts.

If this filter did a perfect job, you'd never have to change oil. Luckily for the oil companies, no filter can trap moisture that condenses in the crankcase, raw fuel that blows by the piston rings, or microscopic particles.

A few years ago bypass type filters were common. About one-tenth of the oil circulated by the pump was filtered. All of the oil is filtered eventually, but an abrasive particle can cause damage on even a single trip through the engine.

Most late-model cars, therefore, use full-flow filters, which clean all the oil in a five-quart system every 25 seconds or so. But when the filter becomes clogged, a relief valve allows the oil to flow around it. This is about as useful as a bypass system with a dirty filter. The engine runs on dirty oil and bearing surfaces, cylinders and the valve train wear faster. That's why the filter cartridge must be changed at least every 6,000 miles with either system. If most of your driving is stop-and-go, in cold weather, or under dusty conditions, replace filters more often.

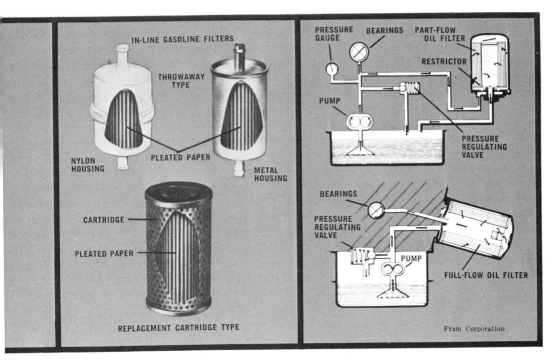

IN-LINE GASOLINE FILTERS

THROWAWAY TYPE

NYLON HOUSING

PLEATED PAPER

METAL HOUSING

CARTRIDGE

PLEATED PAPER

REPLACEMENT CARTRIDGE TYPE

PRESSURE GAUGE    BEARINGS    PART-FLOW OIL FILTER

RESTRICTOR

PUMP

PRESSURE REGULATING VALVE

BEARINGS

PRESSURE REGULATING VALVE

PUMP

FULL-FLOW OIL FILTER

Fram Corporation

**GASOLINE FILTERS** are found on most new cars. Bypass oil filter (top right) cleans some of the oil all of the time, but the full-flow type (bottom) cleans it all every 25 seconds.

On many cars the filter is found right under the hood. On others, you've got to work from underneath the car. Some filters have cartridges that screw on and off. Others slip into screw-top canisters. Whenever you change a cartridge, add an extra quart of oil to replace the oil removed with the old cartridge. Then let the engine idle for several seconds and check for leaks around the filter. Also peek at the pressure gauge or warning light to be sure the oil pump is working.

**Which filter** should you use? Fram, AC, Purolator and Chrysler/Mo-Par all make and recommend pleated paper replacement cartridges. Ford recommends their own cotton-filled filter. It's so efficient that a small opening has been built into it to assure adequate oil pressure to the engine. This cartridge, therefore, suffers from the same drawbacks as a bypass system.

Over the years, many unusual and questionable filters have been offered to the public as replacements for the factory system. One, made of porous bronze, was claimed to last a lifetime. Most engineers don't take it seriously. They say it doesn't filter as well as throwaway types, doesn't hold as much dirt and is hard to clean. And it's so restrictive it can only be used in a bypass system.

Most controversial is a unit that uses an ordinary roll of toilet paper (modestly referred to as T.P. in some ads). Besides the obvious economic advantage—10 to 15 cents a roll versus several dollars for a conventional cartridge—the manufacturers claim their filters are so efficient they can eliminate oil changes.

Those who tested such units say that toilet paper has poor wet strength! Condensation in the oil could make it disintegrate. One engineer agreed that a new roll of toilet paper actually could pick up finer particles of dirt than a conventional cartridge. But this is a mixed blessing. It causes the toilet roll to plug faster. Yet such filters are being used by a number of major corporations, mostly in special-purpose industrial engines,

TOILET PAPER is filter medium in this oil filter system. Inexpensive (10¢ a roll), engineers are still debating its worth.

and they seem to be satisfied with them.

But even if such filters do live up to their startling claims, be warned that you risk losing your engine warranty when you use one. Most manufacturers void their warranties if a mechanical failure is caused by the installation of nonstandard equipment. Trying to prove that your T.P. cartridge wasn't responsible could be tricky and time-consuming.

**All late U.S. cars** and most foreign models have oil filters as standard equipment. Bolt-on, bypass filter kits are available at auto supply stores for early model cars. Prices run from $3 to $15. Full-flow systems, which are built into the block, aren't practical for after-market installation.

**The carburetor air cleaner** removes airborne dirt and dust from the air before it is mixed with the fuel. About 10,000 gallons of dust-laden air pass through the air cleaner for *every* gallon of gasoline burned.

An air cleaner that allows these particles to get through will result in early wear to the upper piston rings and cylinder walls. A clogged air cleaner, on the other hand, restricts the amount of air the carburetor can suck in, causing

an extra rich mixture that cuts performance and gas mileage. If the air cleaner collects enough dirt to plug up completely, the engine won't run at all.

All available air cleaners are serviced by removing either a top cover plate or the entire air cleaner. Most are secured by a threaded stud passing through the center and a wing nut that can be unscrewed by hand. A few require a screwdriver or wrench.

**Air cleaners with pleated** paper cartridges do the best job and are easiest to service. You simply replace the dirty cartridge with a new one.

Polyurethane foam cartridges, if properly maintained, filter nearly as well as paper, but they're not as good at silencing the hiss of air entering the carburetor. Their big advantage is economy: the cartridge can be rinsed in a solvent such as kerosene or carbon tetrachloride, oiled, and reused. The oil forms a tacky trap for dust particles. Allow excess oil to run off before installation. If this sounds like more trouble than it's worth, pleated paper units are available as replacements for many polyurethane models.

Wire-mesh air cleaners are popular on sports and other high performance cars because they allow maximum air flow to the carburetor. They too can be rinsed in solvent, oiled and reused. But they serve more as a fire-arrester than as a filter, allowing everything but small

PRESENT DAY air cleaner of polyurethane foam can be reused indefinitely. It's cleaned in kerosene or carbon tetrachloride.

birds to get through. And they offer no silencing at all.

The once popular oil-bath air cleaner is found mostly on heavy, off-the-highway construction equipment today. Although it has a great capacity for dirt, it isn't as efficient as paper or polyurethane and servicing it is an extremely messy job.

No matter what type of air cleaner you have, it should be inspected every 6,000 miles or six months and replaced or cleaned as necessary—usually every 10,000 to 15,000 miles or every year. In dusty areas, such as the southwest, or in highly industrial areas, more frequent servicing is needed.

**Fuel filters,** considered a luxury a few years ago, are installed on nearly all new cars today. Even so, according to Purolator, last year service stations performed about 33 million carburetor jobs, from cleaning to complete rebuilding. Proper fuel filter maintenance would have made most of those jobs unnecessary.

**Some fuel filters,** known as the in-line type, are spliced into the fuel line between the fuel pump and the carburetor. Others are merely simple metal or nylon screens built into the carburetor. All keep dirt from entering the carburetor and fouling the needle valve and other sensitive parts.

Most in-line filters are replaced entirely when they become dirty. All you need do is loosen the fuel line clamps and pull out the filter nipples. Some filters have removable bronze, paper or ceramic elements. It doesn't pay to clean these elements, as replacements are so inexpensive.

The screen built into the carburetor can be reached by undoing the fuel line at the carburetor inlet. Remove the screen from the brass fitting, rinse in a solvent and replace.

**Fuel filters should be replaced** or serviced at least every 5,000 miles, or twice a year. If they are neglected, the element builds up a coating of dirt dense enough to limit fuel flow, causing the engine to miss at high speed or during hard acceleration. Eventually the engine will stall.

If your engine has no fuel filter, you can install an in-line type easily. Just cut out a short piece of the fuel line near the carburetor, insert the filter ends and secure with clamps or a flanging tool. If your car has a metal fuel line, you'll need a tubing cutter and two short lengths of flexible hose. Force the hose over the metal line and filter nipples and secure with clamps.

**The crankcase breather cap,** according to one AC engineer, is the most neglected filter of all. It's actually an oil filler cap with a clump of metal or synthetic mesh inside. Its job is to clean the air that sweeps through the crankcase to clean out combustion chamber blow-by and condensation. If this filter becomes plugged, it keeps ventilating air from entering the crankcase. This leads to dilution of engine oil and formation of acid, varnish and sludge. It may also allow dirt to enter crankcase.

Servicing this filter is easy. Caps containing metal or "horsehair" mesh must be removed in one piece and cleaned in solvent, dried thoroughly and oiled. Paper and polyurethane units are simply replaced. Ideally, the filter should be serviced at each oil change.

Much of the credit for the longer life of today's engines goes to our modern, improved filters. Giving these filters proper service is the best insurance you can give your engine. •

MOST NEGLECTED of all filters is the oil filler cap. The cap should be cleaned in a solvent regularly, dried thoroughly, oiled.

# MAKE YOUR CAR REALLY THEFT-PROOF!

ABOVE—The speaker and siren-module box are placed in a convenient location under the hood and wired to the switches. BELOW—The switch protecting battery and engine is mounted near the grille.

*A blood-curdling siren and all-points protection give you what plain insurance never could!*

YOU probably spend $10 to $25 a year to insure against the loss of your car by theft. Yet you don't have full coverage. You may have nursed the engine and polished the body and filled the scratches; in fact, you may have the finest car in the world. But if it's stolen all you'll get is ACV—Actual Cash Value —the same amount the guy down the block will get for his car (the one with the loose engine mounts, worn rings, bald tires, bent bumpers and mashed fenders). The insurance companies make no allowance for loving care.

And most likely you don't have inside theft. Can you collect if someone lifts the week's shopping out of your car, the suits you were taking to the cleaners or the luggage you'd packed for the weekend jaunt? Most likely not—few persons carry inside theft (burglary) insurance.

**But if you're willing** to go for a one-shot expense of less than $20 you can protect *fully* against both theft of the car and theft of its contents. The secret is an Auto Theft & Burglar Alarm. No,

it isn't another gadget that blows the car horn if someone sits on the fender. Nor does it blow the horn, which everyone ignores, anyway, as the thief drives off with your pride and joy. Nor is it one of those gadgets that protects against everything but a thief who opens the door or trunk and removes everything in sight. The Theft & Burglar Alarm gives full *siren* protection against the opening of any door or the trunk or the hood, as well as protecting the ignition. And the system locks. Once the siren is tripped it keeps sounding until you reset.

**Our drawings** show the electric circuit. The siren itself consists of a completely assembled electronic siren module connected to a weatherproof speaker. The on-off switch either can be a fender-mounted key switch or a standard DPST toggle concealed behind the grille.

The siren is tripped when the siren module's ground circuit is completed. For example, if the ignition is turned on the relay in the module will close,

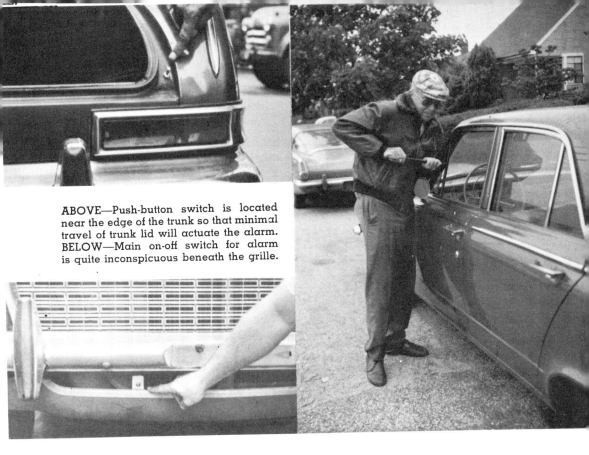

ABOVE—Push-button switch is located near the edge of the trunk so that minimal travel of trunk lid will actuate the alarm. BELOW—Main on-off switch for alarm is quite inconspicuous beneath the grille.

grounding a terminal, and the siren will begin wailing. Similarly, since this terminal also is connected to the car's courtesy-light switches, opening either door will trip the siren (if the main DPST switch is closed).

To get additional protection for the rear doors, trunk, hood and tailgate, it's only necessary to install a push-button switch cut into the courtesy-light circuit. The push-button switches are standard auto door switches available from most new-car dealers. The switches are self-grounding. You need only connect a single wire to the courtesy-light circuit. The siren module (see Parts List) is a bit of an oddity because it *isn't* stocked by the mail-order houses but *is* sold by most electronic-supply stores. Just ask for a siren module.

Don't try to eliminate the relays by changing the switch connections. One relay provides the holding action—once the alarm is tripped it keeps the siren on until the switch is turned off.

**The entire alarm** (except for the

speaker) is assembled in a 3x4x5-in. aluminum cabinet. The siren module is retained by a half-in.-wide aluminum strap, bent as shown. To avoid shorting the module's terminals, wrap several turns of plastic tape around the top of the strap.

Build the alarm exactly as shown. The same circuit should be used for either 6- or 12-volt vehicles. The only difference is in the relay coils. Select either the 6- or 12-volt models from the Parts List.

Mount the alarm and speaker under the hood with the speaker toward the grille for maximum sound dispersal. Double-check that the alarm is grounded to the car body. If necessary scrape away the body paint at the mounting screws.

Complete the installation by connecting the switches, etc., as shown.

**To activate the alarm,** make certain all doors are closed, then close the switch. If anyone opens a door or tries to crawl through a window and jump the ignition the siren will begin its wail

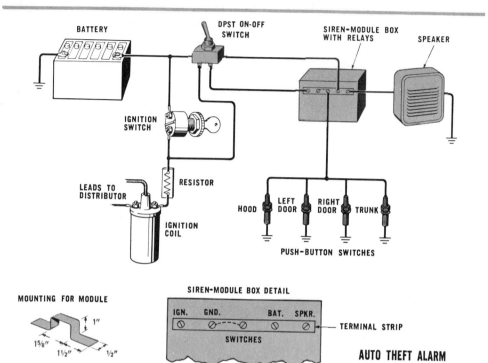

BATTERY

DPST ON-OFF SWITCH

SIREN-MODULE BOX WITH RELAYS

SPEAKER

IGNITION SWITCH

LEADS TO DISTRIBUTOR

RESISTOR

IGNITION COIL

HOOD  LEFT DOOR  RIGHT DOOR  TRUNK

PUSH-BUTTON SWITCHES

MOUNTING FOR MODULE

1"

1 5/8"   1 1/2"   1/2"

SIREN-MODULE BOX DETAIL

IGN.   GND.          BAT.  SPKR.

TERMINAL STRIP

SWITCHES

**AUTO THEFT ALARM**

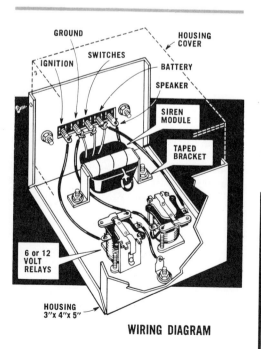

GROUND

HOUSING COVER

IGNITION

SWITCHES

BATTERY

SPEAKER

SIREN MODULE

TAPED BRACKET

6 or 12 VOLT RELAYS

HOUSING 3"x 4"x 5"

**WIRING DIAGRAM**

## Theft-Proof Your Car

as soon as the door is opened or the ignition is jumped. The alarm then can be stopped only by opening the switch or cutting the wires under the hood. Since no dashboard wires are used for the alarm it cannot be stopped from inside the car.

A final note—just be sure to turn off the alarm before *you* get into the car. •

### Parts List

**Relays**—6 volts, Potter & Brumfield RS5D6, Allied Radio 75U986.
12 volts, Potter & Brumfield RS5D12, Allied Radio 75U504 (see text).

**DPST toggle switch**—See text.

**Speaker**—Outdoor weatherproof speaker, Lafayette Radio 44R5201

**Misc.**—Standard Cordover siren module (see text); 3 x 4 x 5-in. cabinet, Lafayette 12R8372; courtesy-light switches as necessary; terminal strip, Lafayette 32R7804

# SIX-STEP SPRING TUNE UP

A LITTLE bit of extra care can make the difference between a tune up that pays off in easy starting, good performance and better gas mileage—and one that makes you wonder why you spent the time and money.

Your present tune up may consist of cleaning or replacing spark plugs and breaker points and adjusting the carburetor's idle. The professional-touch tune up includes these jobs—done somewhat differently—and several other services. All told, a total of six steps.

**One**—Let's begin with the breaker points. Set the gap with a feeler gauge and tighten the setscrew (on all but the GM V-8s, which have a self-locking adjusting screw).

Using a felt-tip marker or piece of chalk, mark the cam lobe on which the rubbing block is resting.

Now crank the engine a couple of times and line up the rubbing block with the cam lobe. Check with a feeler gauge to see that the point gap hasn't become smaller.

If it has, you've uncovered a source of trouble since point spacing affects coil output and ignition timing. Usually the problem is a loose setscrew because either the lock washer was left out or you didn't tighten it adequately in the first place.

If the screw won't hold due to a stripped thread, replace the screw or breaker-point retaining plate (commonly called the breaker plate). If the points are being held in place, the problem is in a major component of the distributor (cam or cam bushing) and a rebuilt distributor may be necessary.

The engine still may perform to your satisfaction, particularly if the variation in point gap is small, .003 in. or less. But be warned: even a small variation may cause the engine to miss, especially if the condition of the ignition system is only fair in other respects (condition of coil, resistor and connections, etc.).

**Two**—If you're cleaning and regap-

TIGHTEN setscrew on breaker points after setting the gap to original specifications. Then run engine, stop and check again.

REMOVE, inspect filter. Clean polyurethane foam elements in solvent and oil baths. Replace, don't clean, pleated paper elements.

109

ping the plugs, use a small, flat file to flatten the electrode firing surfaces. Normal wear tends to round off the center electrode and dish the inside of the side electrode. Careful filing will reduce the voltage required to fire the plug and might cure or prevent a high-speed miss.

**Three**—Take off the air filter and inspect it. A dirty air filter reduces air intake, which in turn reduces high-speed performance and gas mileage (a dirty air filter can be responsible for mileage drops up to 30 per cent).

Most late-model cars are equipped with an air-filter element made of pleated, resin-impregnated, multi-layer cellulose (commonly called filter paper). Others have a polyurethane-foam element.

Pleated paper element service is a snap. As soon as the element is visibly dirty, discard it and install a new one. Normally the replacement interval is 10,000 to 15,000 mi.

The polyurethane-foam element can be cleaned, although you can't expect too much in the way of results. Soak the element in solvent, squeeze it out and allow it to dry. Then dunk it in clean engine oil and again squeeze out the excess.

For reasonable results this should be done every 3,000 to 4,000 mi. Or you can

discard the polyurethane and install a paper filter, which also is made as a replacement for the polyurethane.

While the air filter is off, check the position of the choke and its mechanical linkage. If the engine is cold the choke plate should cover the carburetor air horn. If the engine is warm the choke plate should be close to vertical (check the plate under both conditions). Also move the plate back and forth to make sure it isn't binding.

With the engine cold, open the throttle all the way by pulling the linkage at the carburetor or have someone floor the gas pedal. The choke plate should crack open a fraction of an inch if the linkage is set properly (failure of the choke to crack open will prevent the engine from breathing properly at highway speeds while still cold). If the choke isn't performing as it should, don't try a carburetor adjustment. If you can't fix the choke yourself, give the job to someone who can.

**Four**—Disconnect the fuel line at the carburetor and if there is a filter element in the carburetor inlet, service it as part of the tune up. Paper elements are replaced; sintered bronze and wire screens are cleaned in carburetor solvent.

There also should be a filter with a pleated paper element clamped either

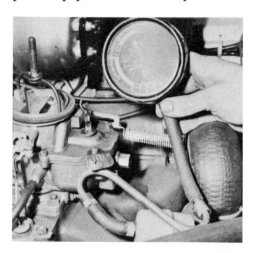

OPEN the throttle by pulling linkage. The choke should crack open a fraction of an inch. If not, see a carburetor specialist.

CONNECT a fuel-pressure gauge to the fuel line. Start the engine and run it on fuel in carb. This checks pressure, cleans carb.

into the fuel line or on the outlet side of the fuel pump. This filter should be replaced at least once a year. A clogged or severely restricted fuel filter can cause fuel starvation.

With a new filter in the line and the line disconnected, attach a fuel-pressure gauge to the end. Start the engine, running it on the fuel still in the carburetor bowl.

This accomplishes two things. First, it permits a check of fuel-pump pressure with the engine running. (A weak fuel pump or a restricted or kinked fuel line can cause fuel starvation.)

Secondly, when the line is reconnected and the engine is cranked, the empty fuel bowl will accept fuel as fast as it can be delivered. The inrushing gasoline will wash slime from around the float needle and seat assembly (these regulate gasoline flow into the bowl). Excessive slime can hold the float needle valve open when the bowl is full, permitting extra gasoline to pour in and flood the carburetor.

**Five**—Many late-model cars are equipped with a Positive Crankcase Ventilation (PCV) system that directs crankcase vapors into the cylinders to reduce air pollution.

A spring-loaded vacuum-regulated valve is used in the design of the typical system. Unless the valve is cleaned periodically and replaced annually, it may malfunction and cause, among other things, stalling, rough idle and buildup of crankcase pressure (with damage to oil seals and gaskets resulting).

Special solvents in spout cans are available for cleaning of the valve. Their simplicity makes them especially suitable for week-end-mechanic use.

With the engine off, disconnect the hose at the crankcase. (On most cars, the hose runs from the base of the carburetor to the rocker cover, with the valve built into the end at the rocker cover.)

Push the spout of the solvent container against the valve, forcing it open. Squirt solvent into the valve and work the solvent into the innards of the valve by pushing the valve open against the spring. Allow it to open and close several times.

Allow a few minutes for the solvent to soak in. Start the engine and squirt a bit more solvent into the end of the hose. Reconnect the hose, run the engine at a fast idle for a few minutes and the job is done.

**Six**—Now you can warm up the engine and prepare to set the idle. Because the engine should be warm, this job should be attempted only after a drive of at least 20 minutes.

Begin by identifying the idle mixture screws in the base of the carburetor (four-barrel carbs have two mixture screws). To set each screw (which controls fuel flow through the idle passage) turn it in until the engine just starts to stumble, then turn it out. Do this slowly and the engine will smooth out and run faster. Half to three quarters of a turn should be adequate.

If the adjustment seems to make no difference in the idle, this indicates dirty idle passages and worn mixture-screw needles (the needles are tapered and are found on the other ends of the adjusting screws). A carburetor cleanout and new screws are dictated.

Once the adjustment goes smoothly check engine speed. If the idle is too fast or too slow after idle-mixture adjustment, reset the throttle stop screw (the adjusting screw on the carburetor linkage to the gas pedal) until the speed is satisfactory.

On cars with alternators, adjust the idle speed with the headlamps turned on. This imposes an electrical load and compensates for the fact that the alternator often may be charging at idle speed. This draws power from the engine, affecting the idle.

If turning the throttle stop screw doesn't seem to change idle speed, make certain that the screw is bearing against the linkage. On some cars with automatic transmission it may be necessary to disconnect the link to the transmission before making the adjustment.

Idle speed, of course, should be set with a tachometer to factory specifications. Without a tach, you really need a professional's ear (which is something that even professionals sometimes won't trust).

If you insist on guessing, however, make certain the idle speed is high enough to turn off the battery charging bulb, yet not so high that the car creeps forward with the shift lever in Drive. •